1 Kum ba yah *traditional*

MELODY

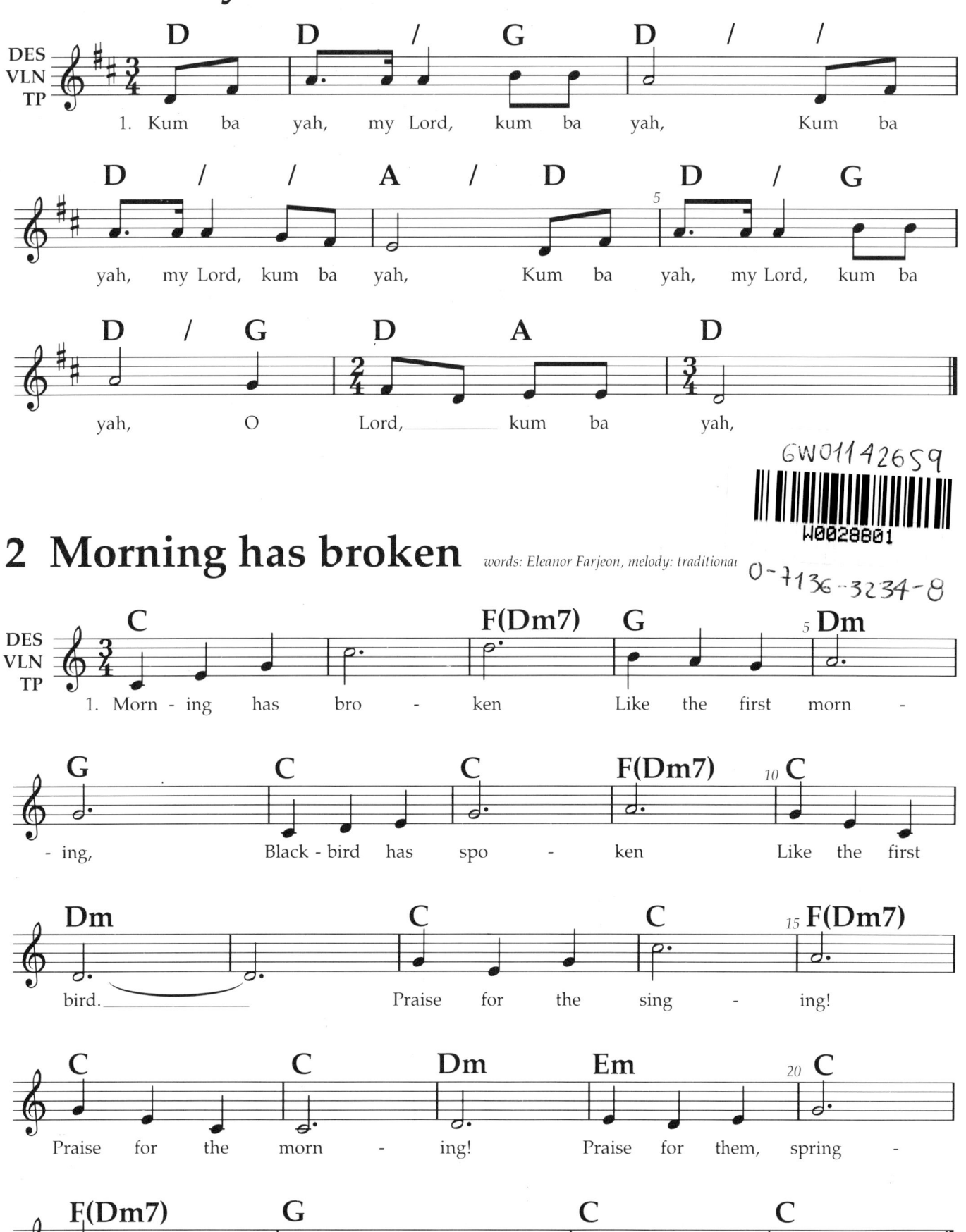

1. Kum ba yah, my Lord, kum ba yah, Kum ba yah, my Lord, kum ba yah, Kum ba yah, my Lord, kum ba yah, O Lord, kum ba yah,

2 Morning has broken

words: Eleanor Farjeon, melody: traditional

1. Morn-ing has bro-ken Like the first morn-ing, Black-bird has spo-ken Like the first bird. Praise for the sing-ing! Praise for the morn-ing! Praise for them, spring-ing Fresh from the Lord!

© 1990, A & C BLACK (PUBLISHERS) LTD

3 Come and praise the Lord our King *traditional*

Introduction

1. Come and praise the Lord our King, Hal-le-lu-jah. Come praise the Lord our King, Hal-le-lu-jah.

Chorus

Christ was born in Beth-le-hem, Hal-le-lu-jah, Son of God and Son of Man, Hal-le-lu-jah.

Last time D. C. al fine

4 All things which live below the sky

words: Edward J. Brailsford, melody: collected and adapted by R. Vaughan Williams

Introduction

1. All things which live be-low the sky, Or move with-in the sea, Are crea-tures of the Lord most high, And bro-thers un-to me.

5 Every star shall sing a carol *Sydney Carter*

1. Every star shall sing a carol; Every creature, high or low,
Come and praise the King of Heaven By whatever name you know.

God above, Man below, Holy is the name I know.

6 Simple gifts *traditional Shaker song*

Introduction

'Tis the gift to be simple, 'tis the gift to be free, 'Tis the gift to come down where you ought to be, And when we find ourselves in the place just right, 'Twill be in the valley of love and delight.

When true simplicity is gained, To bow and to bend we shan't be ashamed; To turn, turn will be our delight, 'Til by turning, turning we come round right.

7 Lord of the harvest
words: Fred Kaan, melody: June Tillman

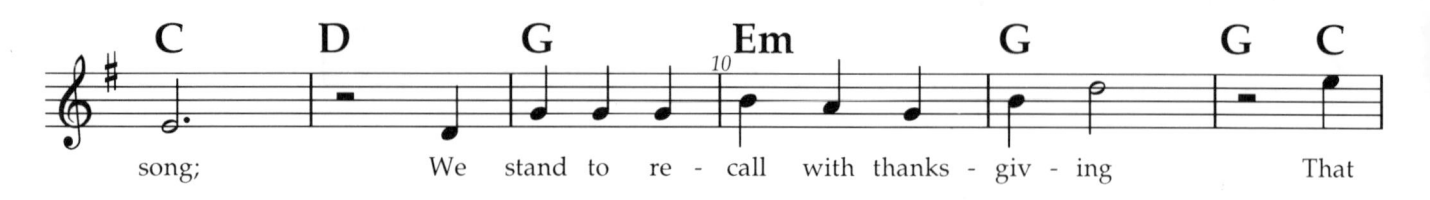

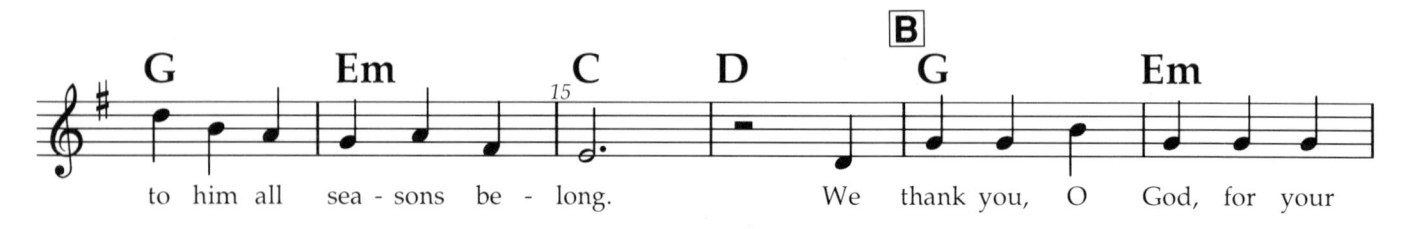

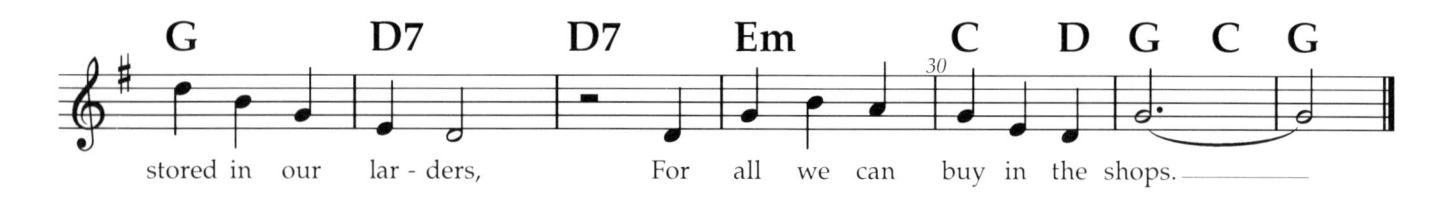

1. Now join we to praise the cre-a-tor, Our voi-ces in wor-ship and song; We stand to re-call with thanks-giv-ing That to him all sea-sons be-long. We thank you, O God, for your good-ness, For the joy and a-bun-dance of crops, For food that is stored in our lar-ders, For all we can buy in the shops.

8 The vine and the fig tree
traditional

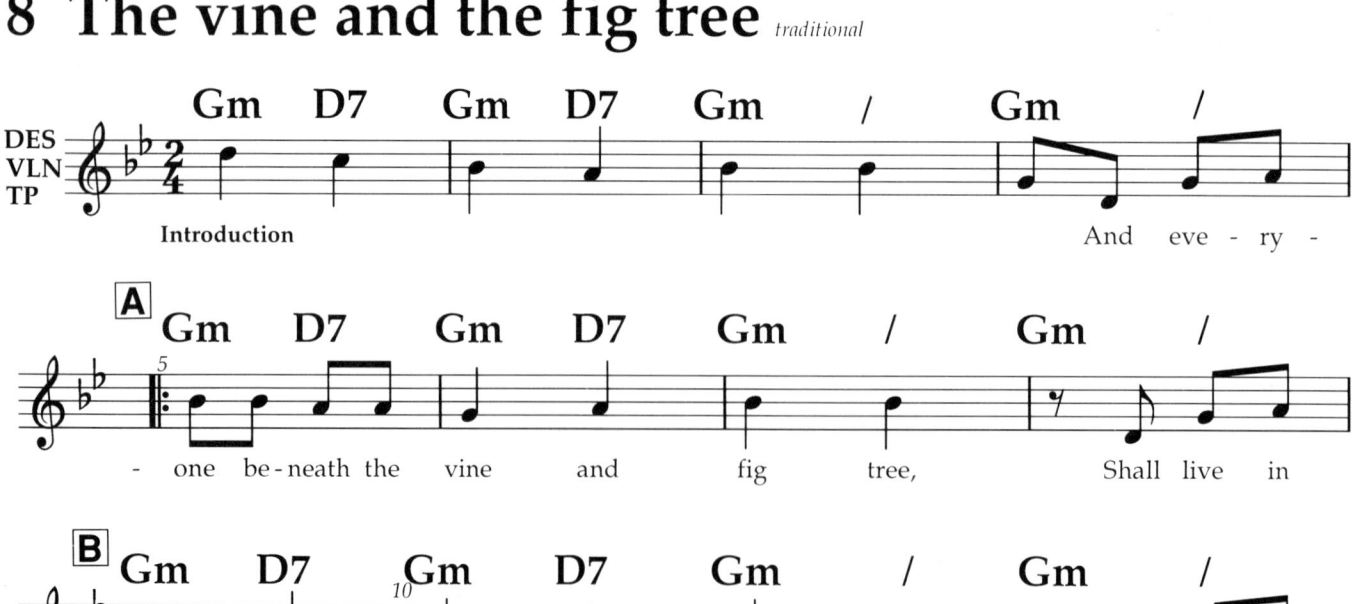

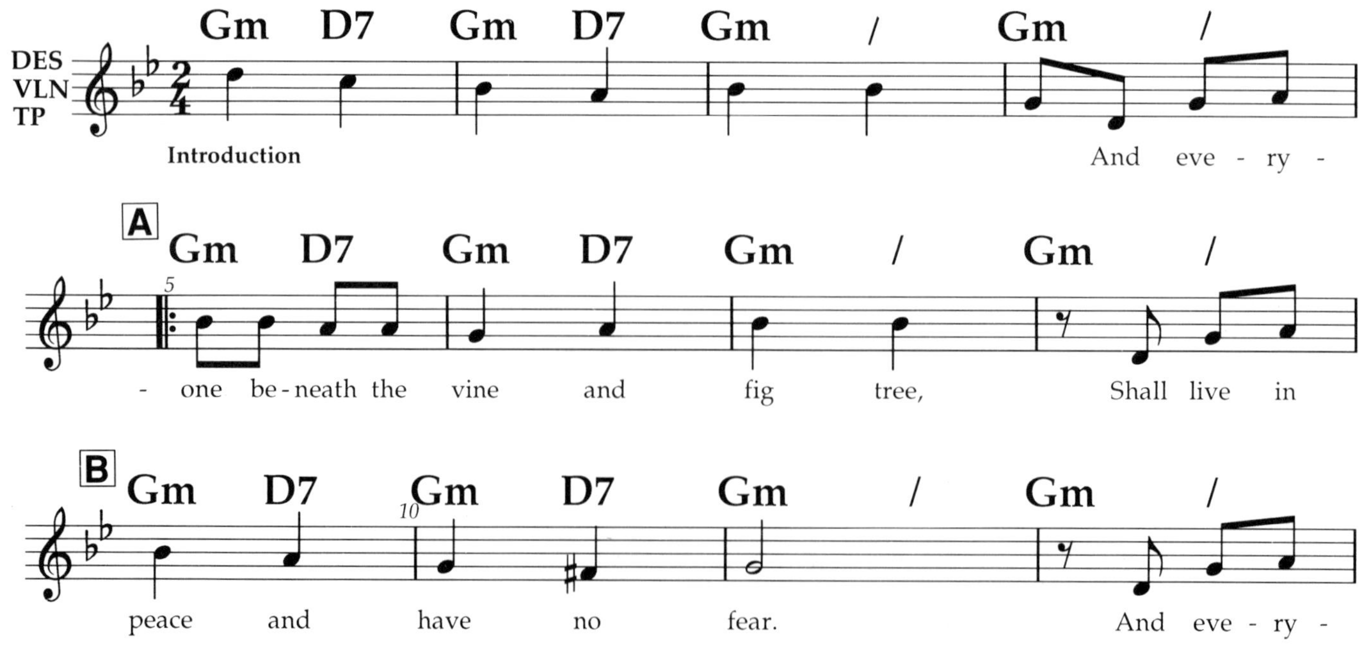

Introduction

And eve-ry-one be-neath the vine and fig tree, Shall live in peace and have no fear. And eve-ry-

[C] -one beneath the vine and fig tree, Shall live in

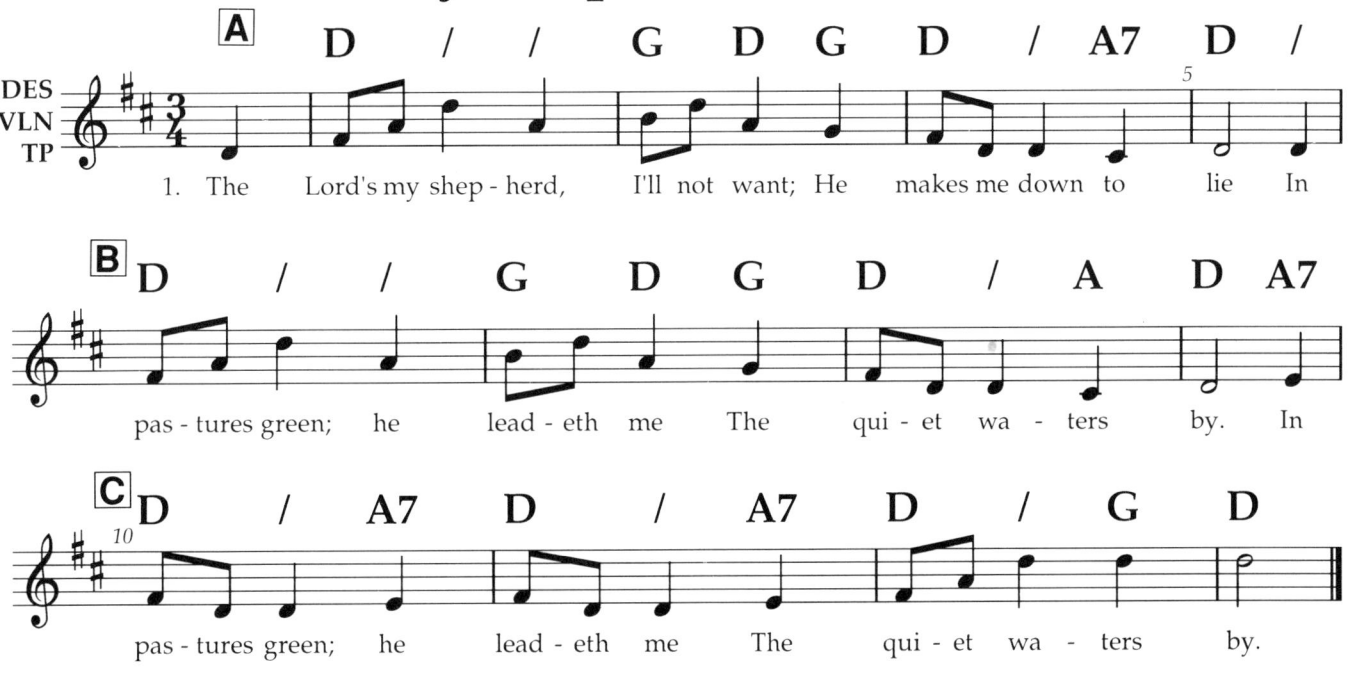

[D] peace and have no fear. *Fine*

[E] And into plough-shares turn their swords,

[F] Nations shall learn war no more.

[G] And into plough-shares turn their swords,

[H] Nations shall learn war no more. And eve-ry- *Repeat from A to fine*

9 The Lord's my shepherd
words: W. Whittingham, melody: J. L. MacBeth Bain

[A] 1. The Lord's my shep-herd, I'll not want; He makes me down to lie In

[B] pas-tures green; he lead-eth me The qui-et wa-ters by. In

[C] pas-tures green; he lead-eth me The qui-et wa-ters by.

10 Lord of the ocean
words: David Harding, melody: (Skye Boat Song) traditional

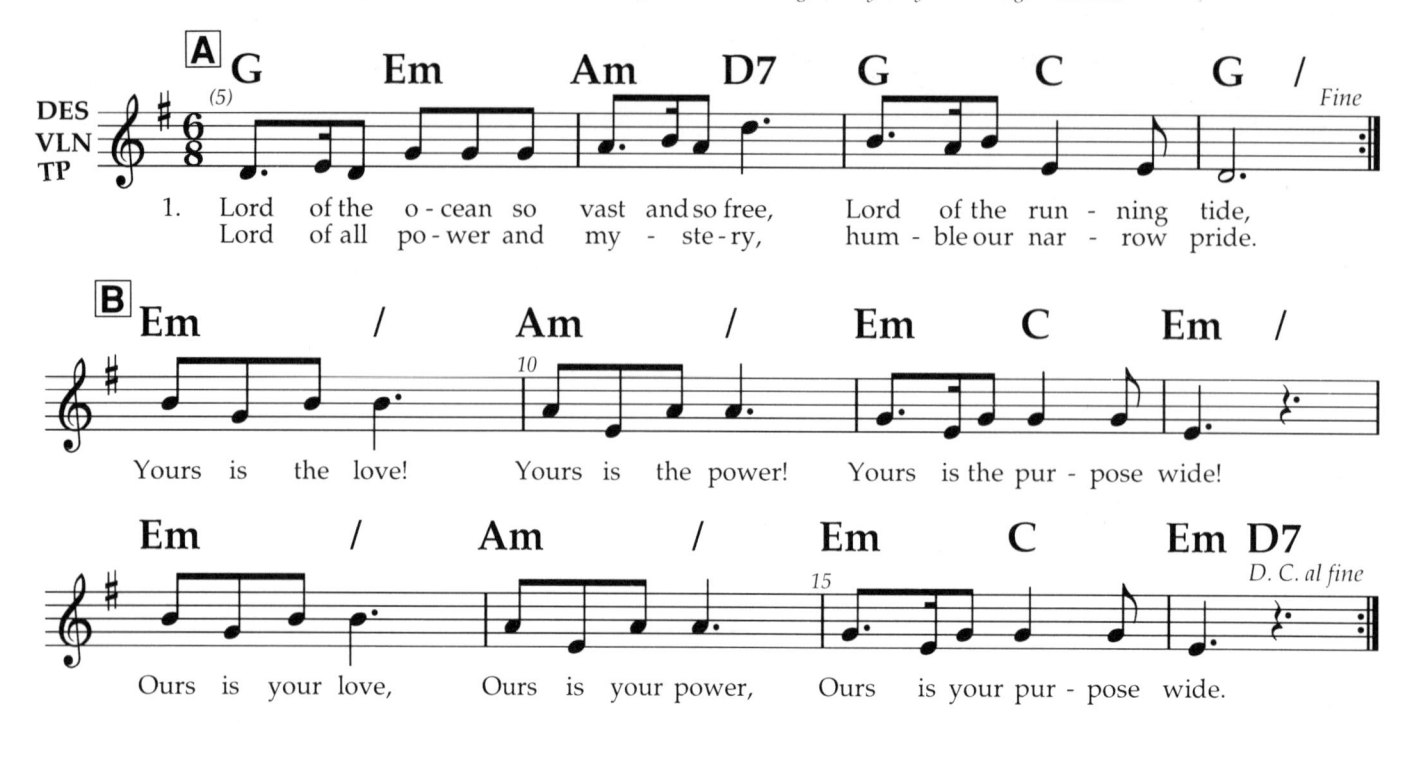

1. Lord of the o-cean so vast and so free, Lord of the run-ning tide,
   Lord of all po-wer and my-ste-ry, hum-ble our nar-row pride.

Yours is the love! Yours is the power! Yours is the pur-pose wide!

Ours is your love, Ours is your power, Ours is your pur-pose wide.

11 Bread and fishes
Alan Bell

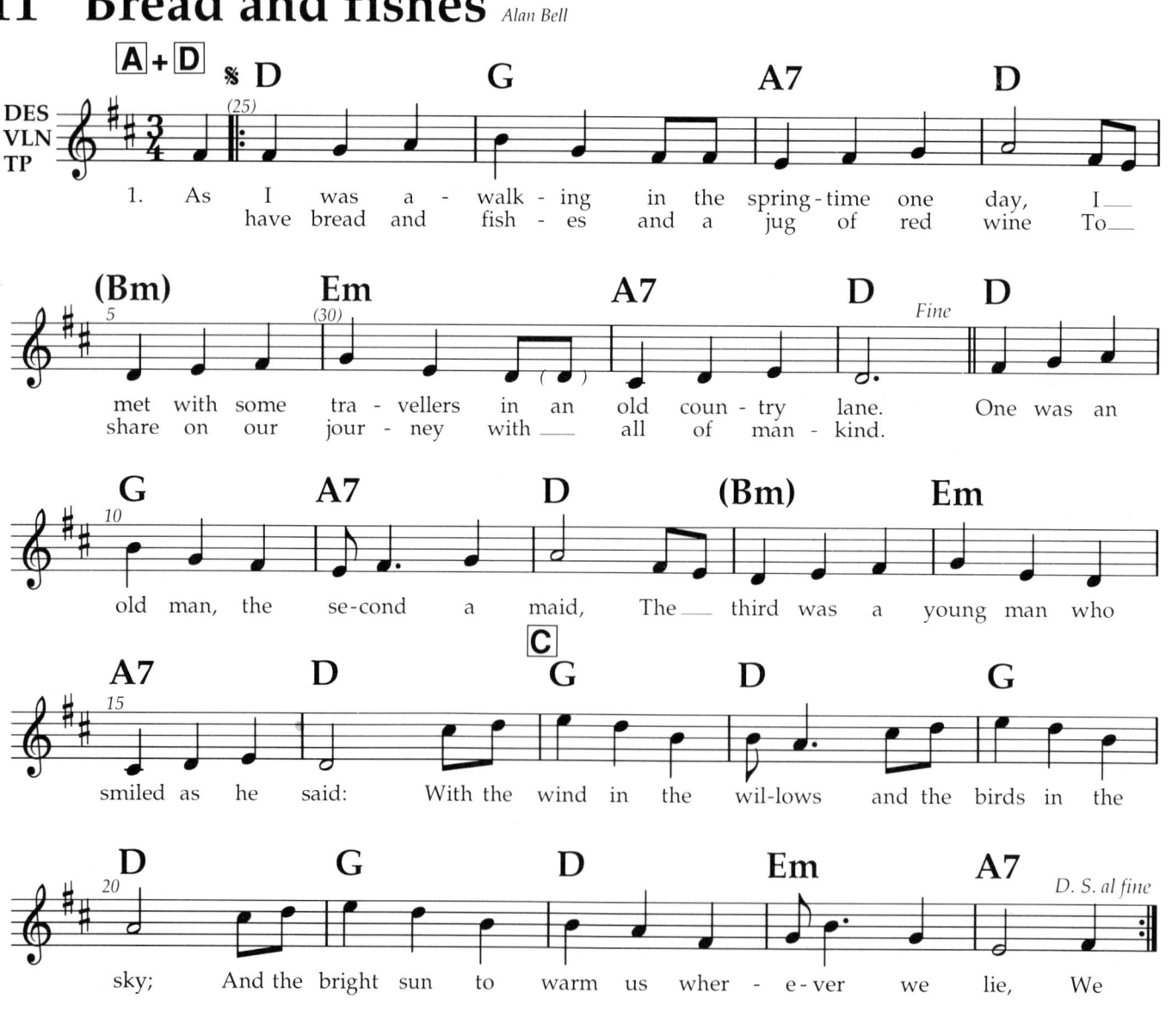

1. As I was a-walk-ing in the spring-time one day, I
   have bread and fish-es and a jug of red wine To

met with some tra-vellers in an old coun-try lane. One was an
share on our jour-ney with all of man-kind.

old man, the se-cond a maid, The third was a young man who

smiled as he said: With the wind in the wil-lows and the birds in the

sky; And the bright sun to warm us wher-e-ver we lie, We

12 Sing hosanna *traditional*

Introduction

1. Give me joy in my heart, keep me praising— Give me joy in my heart, I pray; Give me joy in my heart, Keep me praising,— Keep me praising till the break of day:

Chorus

Sing Hosanna! Sing Hosanna! Sing Hosanna to the King of Kings! Sing Hosanna! Sing Hosanna! Sing Hosanna to the King.

13 The day thou gavest *words: John Ellerton, melody: Clement C. Scholefield*

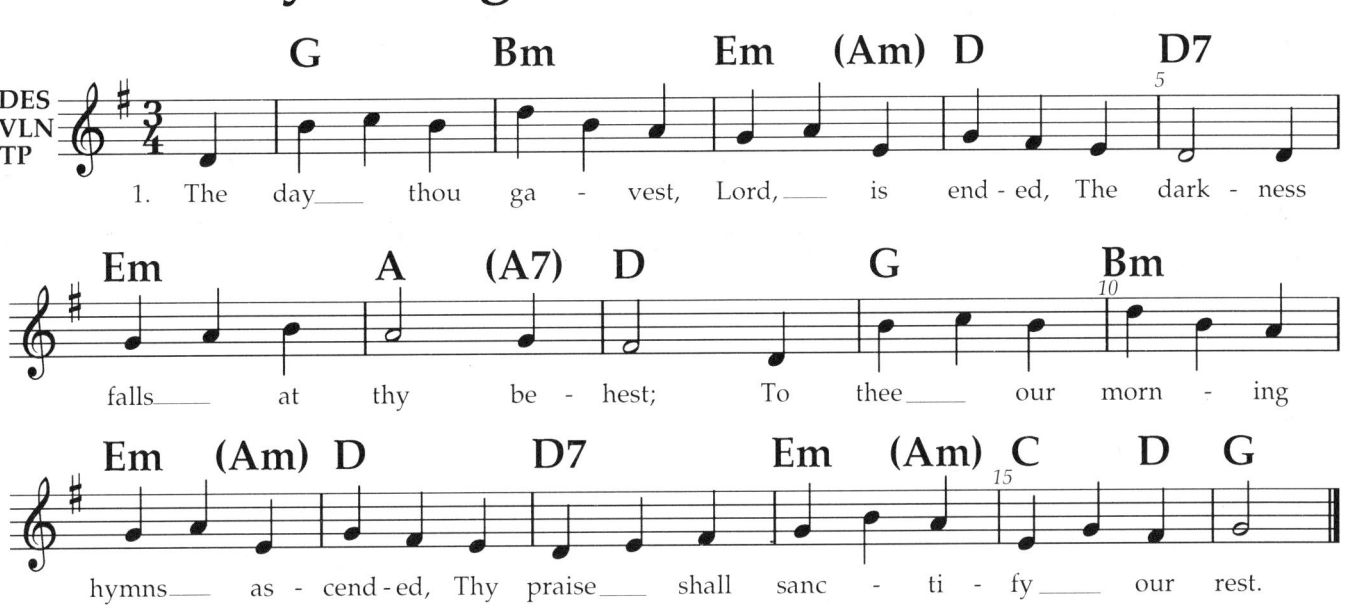

1. The day thou gavest, Lord, is ended, The darkness falls at thy behest; To thee our morning hymns ascended, Thy praise shall sanctify our rest.

14 Make me a channel of your peace
Sebastian Temple

Introduction

1. Make me a chan-nel of your peace. ____ Where there is hat-red, let me bring your love; ____ Where there is in-ju-ry, your par-don, Lord; ____ And where there's doubt, true faith in you. ____ *Fine*

O Mas-ter, grant that I may ne-ver seek ____ So much to be con-soled as to con-sole, ____ To be un-der-stood as to un-der-stand: ____ To be loved, as to love with all my soul. ____ *Repeat A*

The following copyright owners have kindly granted their permission for the reprinting of words and music:

Franciscan Communications for the words and melody of *14 Make me a channel of your peace* by Sebastian Temple.

David Harding for the words of *10 Lord of the ocean*.

David Higham Associates for the words of *2 Morning has broken* by Eleanor Farjeon.

Maypole Music Ltd for the words and melody of *11 Bread and fishes* by Alan Bell.

Oxford University Press for the melody of *4 All things which live below the sky* collected and adapted by R. Vaughan Williams.

Stainer & Bell Ltd and Hope Publishing Co for the words of *7 Lord of the harvest* by Fred Kaan.

Stainer & Bell Ltd and Galaxy Music Corp for the words and melody of *5 Every star shall sing a carol* by Sydney Carter, and the melody of *7 Lord of the harvest*, adapted from a Scottish tune by June Tillman.

1 Kum ba yah *traditional*

MELODY

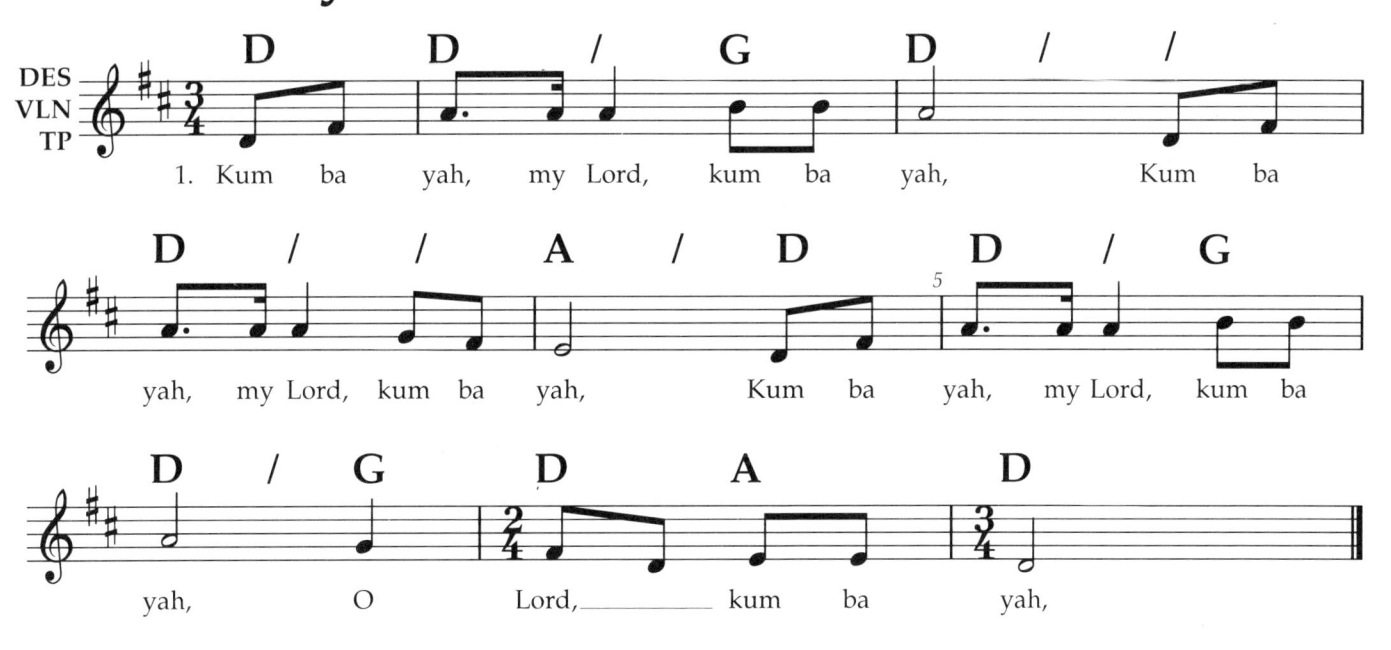

1. Kum ba yah, my Lord, kum ba yah, Kum ba yah, my Lord, kum ba yah, Kum ba yah, my Lord, kum ba yah, O Lord, kum ba yah,

2 Morning has broken *words: Eleanor Farjeon, melody: traditional*

1. Morn-ing has bro-ken Like the first morn-ing, Black-bird has spo-ken Like the first bird. Praise for the sing-ing! Praise for the morn-ing! Praise for them, spring-ing Fresh from the Lord!

© 1990, A & C BLACK (PUBLISHERS) LTD

3 Come and praise the Lord our King *traditional*

Introduction

1. Come and praise the Lord our King, Hal-le-lu-jah. Come praise the Lord our King, Hal-le-lu-jah.

Chorus

Christ was born in Beth-le-hem, Hal-le-lu-jah, Son of God and Son of Man, Hal-le-lu-jah.

Last time D. C. al fine

4 All things which live below the sky

words: Edward J. Brailsford, melody: collected and adapted by R. Vaughan Williams

Introduction

1. All things which live be-low the sky, Or move with-in the sea, Are crea-tures of the Lord most high, And bro-thers un-to me.

5 Every star shall sing a carol *Sydney Carter*

1. Every star shall sing a carol; Every creature, high or low,
Come and praise the King of Heaven By whatever name you know.
God above, Man below, Holy is the name I know.

6 Simple gifts *traditional Shaker song*

Introduction

'Tis the gift to be simple, 'tis the gift to be free, 'Tis the gift to come down where you ought to be, And when we find ourselves in the place just right, 'Twill be in the valley of love and delight.

When true simplicity is gained, To bow and to bend we shan't be ashamed; To turn, turn will be our delight, 'Til by turning, turning we come round right.

7 Lord of the harvest
words: Fred Kaan, melody: June Tillman

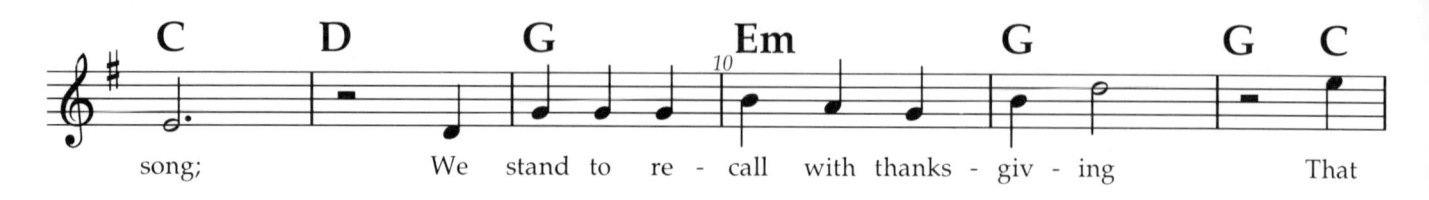

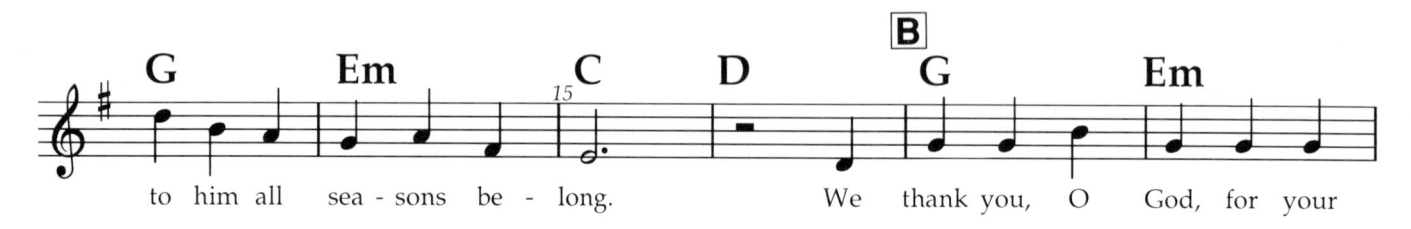

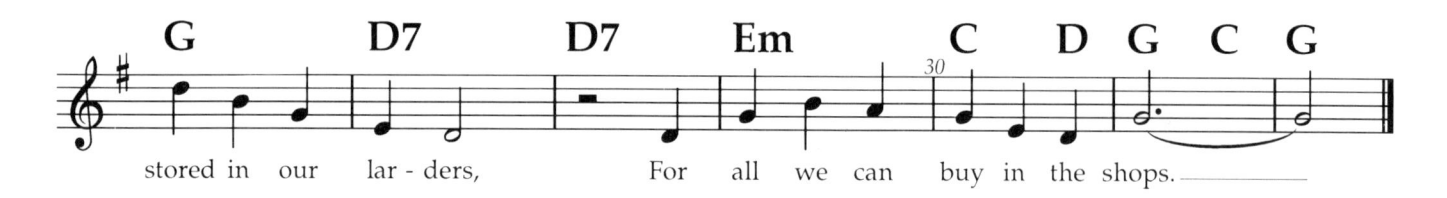

1. Now join we to praise the cre-a-tor, Our voi-ces in wor-ship and song; We stand to re-call with thanks-giv-ing That to him all sea-sons be-long. We thank you, O God, for your good-ness, For the joy and a-bun-dance of crops, For food that is stored in our lar-ders, For all we can buy in the shops.

8 The vine and the fig tree
traditional

Introduction

And eve-ry-one be-neath the vine and fig tree, Shall live in peace and have no fear. And eve-ry-

[C] | Gm D7 | Gm D7 | Gm / | Gm / |

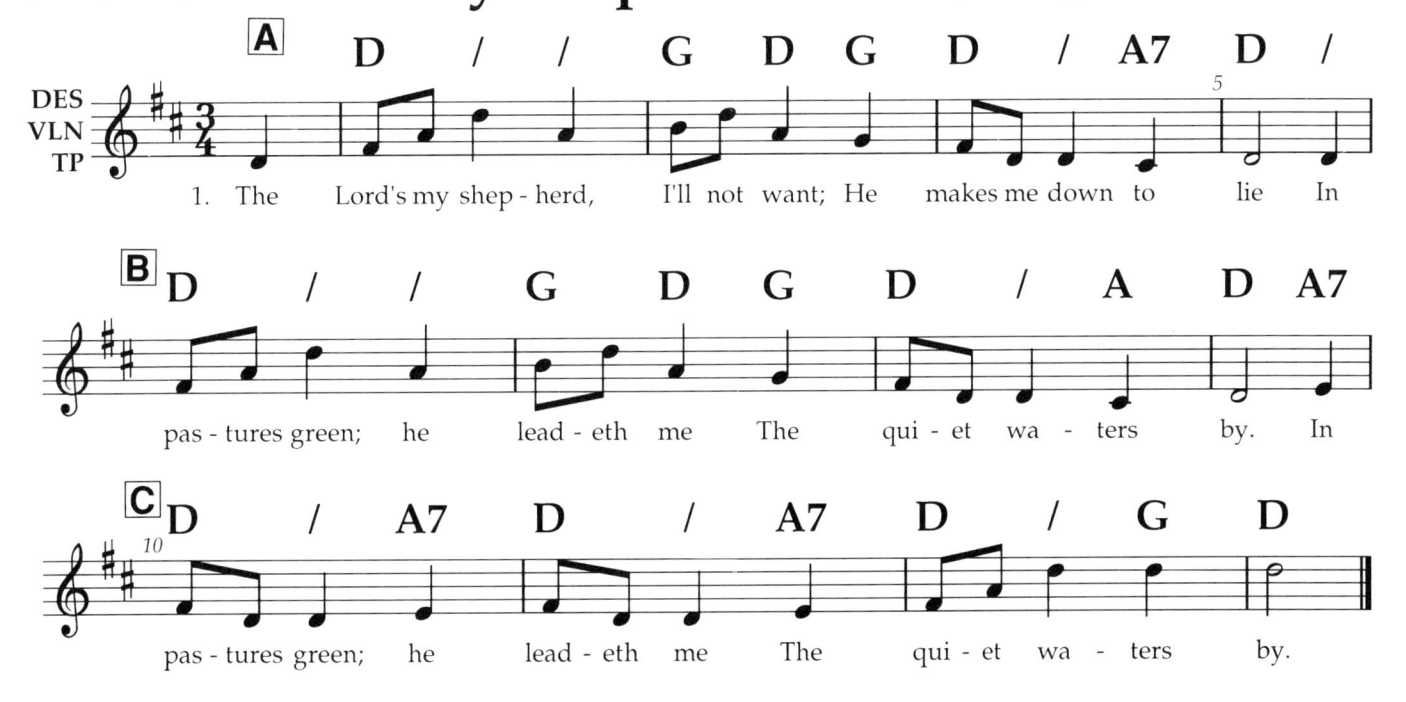

-one beneath the vine and fig tree, Shall live in

[D] | Gm D7 | Gm D7 | Gm / | Gm / | *Fine*

peace and have no fear.

[E] | Gm D7 | Gm D7 | Gm / | Gm / |

And into plough-shares turn their swords,

[F] | Gm D7 | Gm D7 | Gm / | Gm / |

Nations shall learn war no more.

[G] | Gm D7 | Gm D7 | Gm / | Gm / |

And into plough-shares turn their swords,

[H] | Gm D7 | Gm D7 | Gm / | Gm / | *Repeat from A to fine*

Nations shall learn war no more. And every-

9 The Lord's my shepherd
words: W. Whittingham, melody: J. L. MacBeth Bain

[A] | D / / | G D G D / | A7 D / |

DES / VLN / TP

1. The Lord's my shepherd, I'll not want; He makes me down to lie In

[B] | D / / | G D G D / | A D A7 |

pastures green; he leadeth me The quiet waters by. In

[C] | D / A7 D / | A7 D / | G D |

pastures green; he leadeth me The quiet waters by.

10 Lord of the ocean
words: David Harding, melody: (Skye Boat Song) traditional

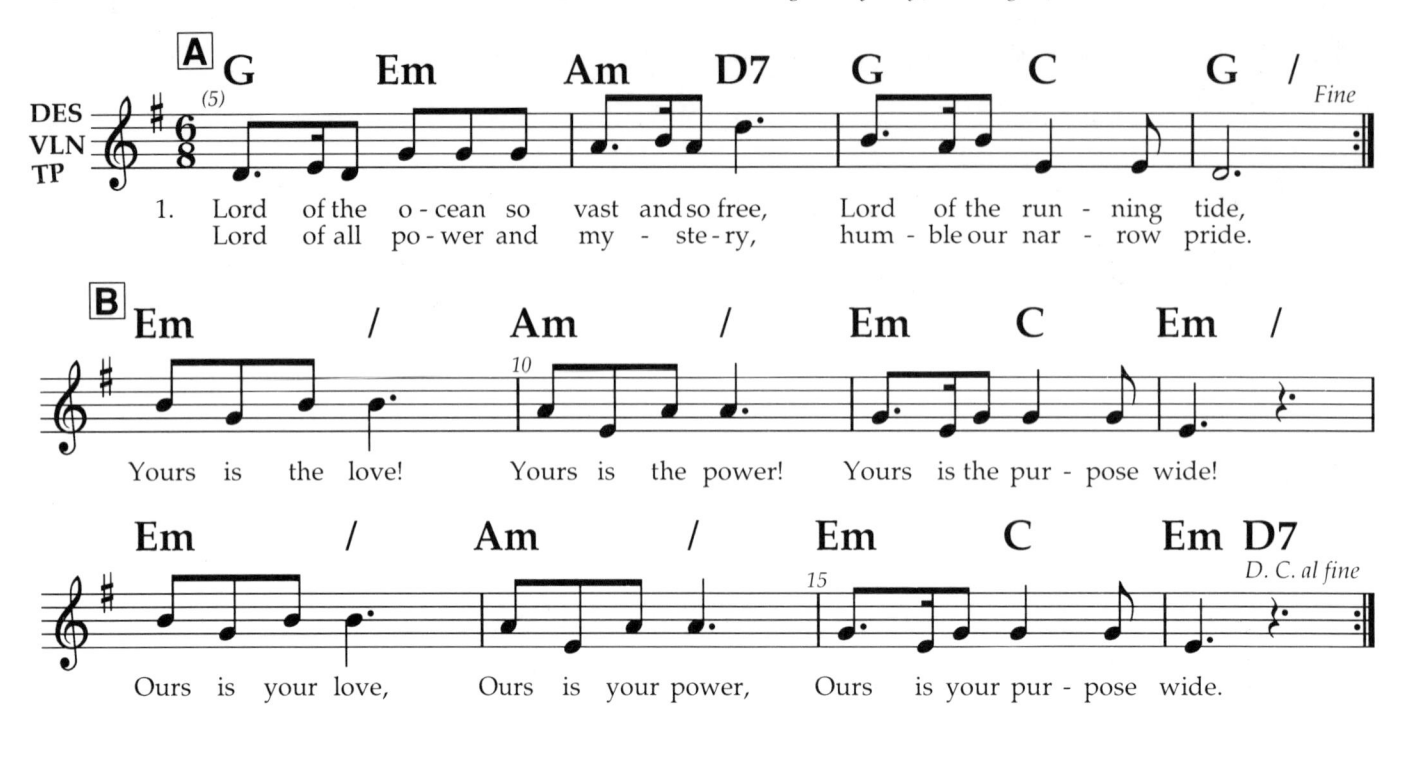

1. Lord of the o-cean so vast and so free, Lord of the run-ning tide,
   Lord of all po-wer and my-ste-ry, hum-ble our nar-row pride.

Yours is the love! Yours is the power! Yours is the pur-pose wide!

Ours is your love, Ours is your power, Ours is your pur-pose wide.

11 Bread and fishes
Alan Bell

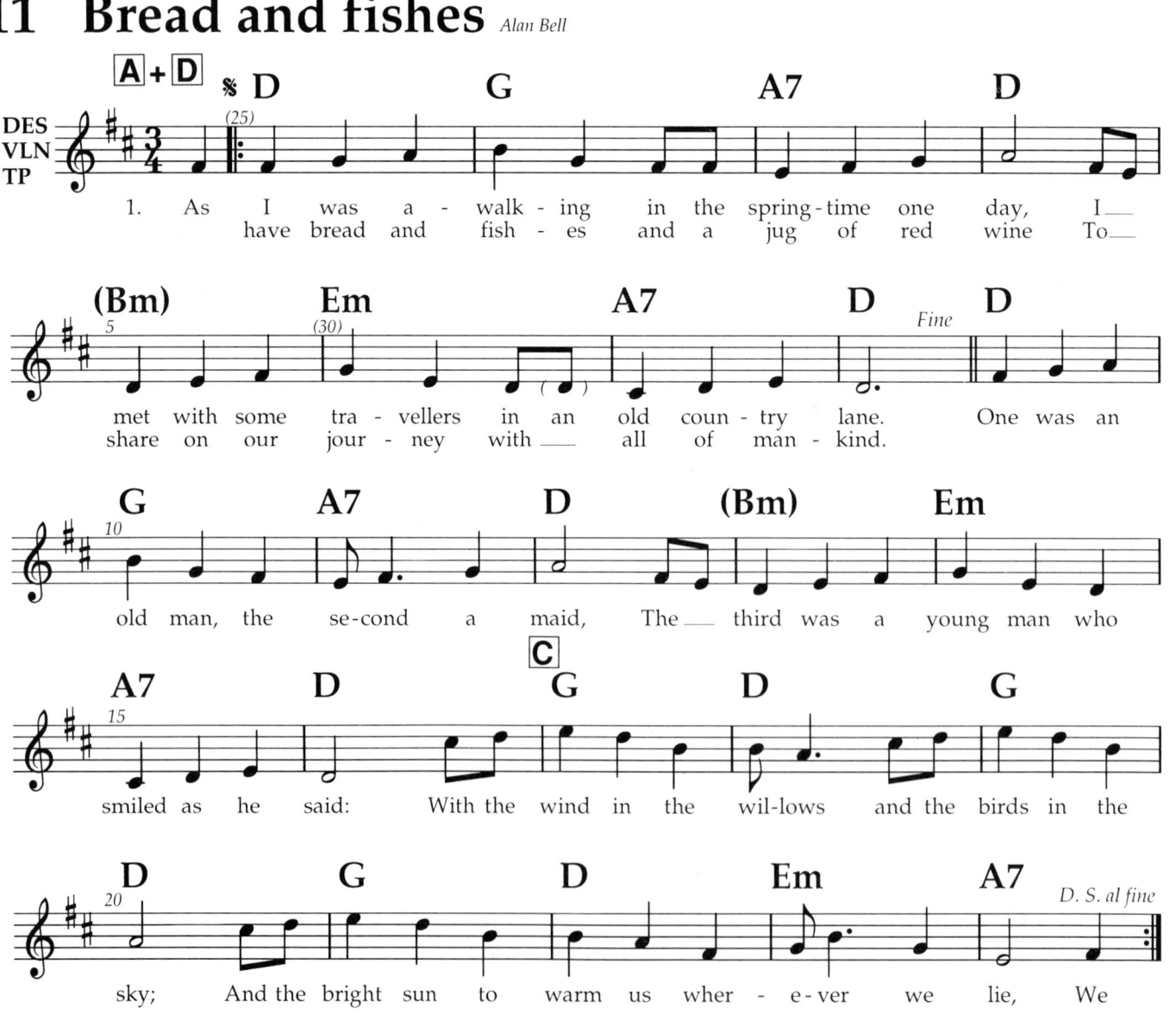

1. As I was a-walk-ing in the spring-time one day, I
   have bread and fish-es and a jug of red wine To

met with some tra-vellers in an old coun-try lane. One was an
share on our jour-ney with all of man-kind.

old man, the se-cond a maid, The third was a young man who

smiled as he said: With the wind in the wil-lows and the birds in the

sky; And the bright sun to warm us wher-e-ver we lie, We

12 Sing hosanna *traditional*

Introduction

1. Give me joy in my heart, keep me prais-ing— Give me joy in my heart, I pray; Give me joy in my heart, Keep me prais-ing,— Keep me prais-ing till the break of day:

Chorus

Sing Ho-san-na! Sing Ho-san-na! Sing Ho-san-na to the King of Kings! Sing Ho-san-na! Sing Ho-san-na! Sing Ho-san-na to the King.

13 The day thou gavest *words: John Ellerton, melody: Clement C. Scholefield*

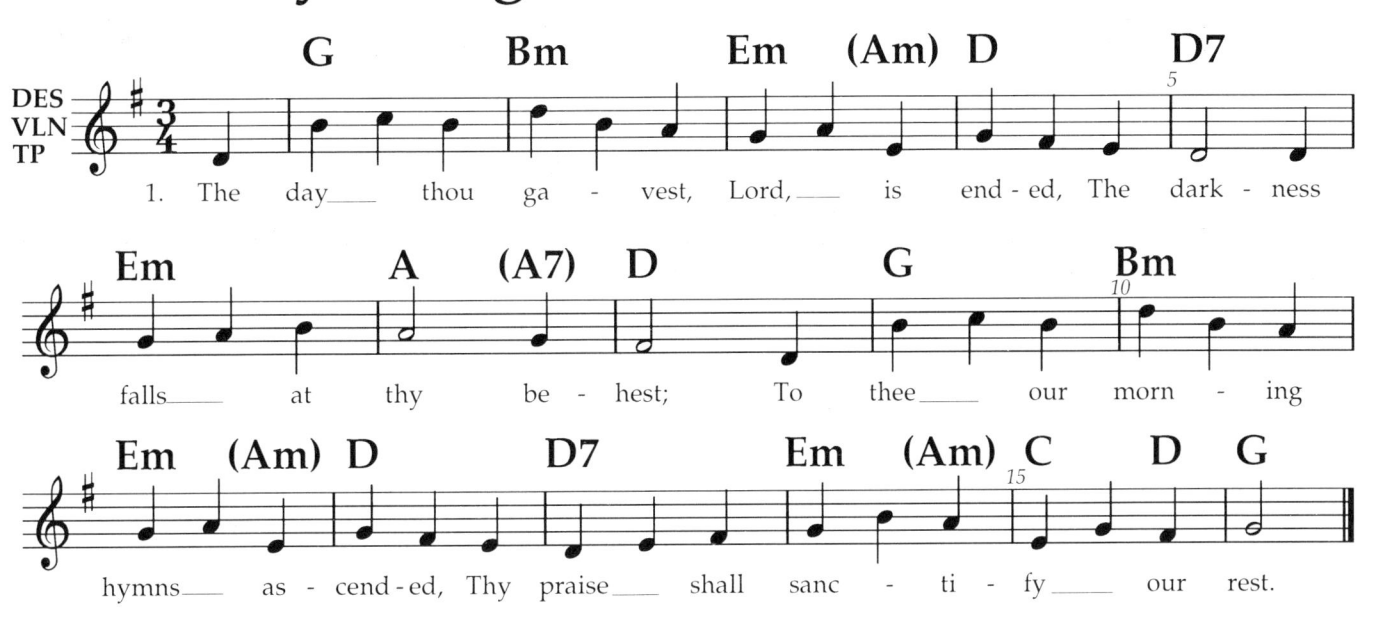

1. The day thou ga-vest, Lord, is end-ed, The dark-ness falls at thy be-hest; To thee our morn-ing hymns as-cend-ed, Thy praise shall sanc-ti-fy our rest.

14 Make me a channel of your peace
Sebastian Temple

Introduction

1. Make me a chan-nel of your peace. _____ Where there is hat-red, let me bring your love; _____ Where there is in-ju-ry, your par-don, Lord; _____ And where there's doubt, true faith in you. _____ O Mas-ter, grant that I may ne-ver seek _____ So much to be con-soled as to con-sole, _____ To be un-der-stood as to un-der-stand: _____ To be loved, as to love with all my soul. _____

The following copyright owners have kindly granted their permission for the reprinting of words and music:

Franciscan Communications for the words and melody of *14 Make me a channel of your peace* by Sebastian Temple.

David Harding for the words of *10 Lord of the ocean*.

David Higham Associates for the words of *2 Morning has broken* by Eleanor Farjeon.

Maypole Music Ltd for the words and melody of *11 Bread and fishes* by Alan Bell.

Oxford University Press for the melody of *4 All things which live below the sky* collected and adapted by R. Vaughan Williams.

Stainer & Bell Ltd and Hope Publishing Co for the words of *7 Lord of the harvest* by Fred Kaan.

Stainer & Bell Ltd and Galaxy Music Corp for the words and melody of *5 Every star shall sing a carol* by Sydney Carter, and the melody of *7 Lord of the harvest*, adapted from a Scottish tune by June Tillman.

1 Kum ba yah *traditional*

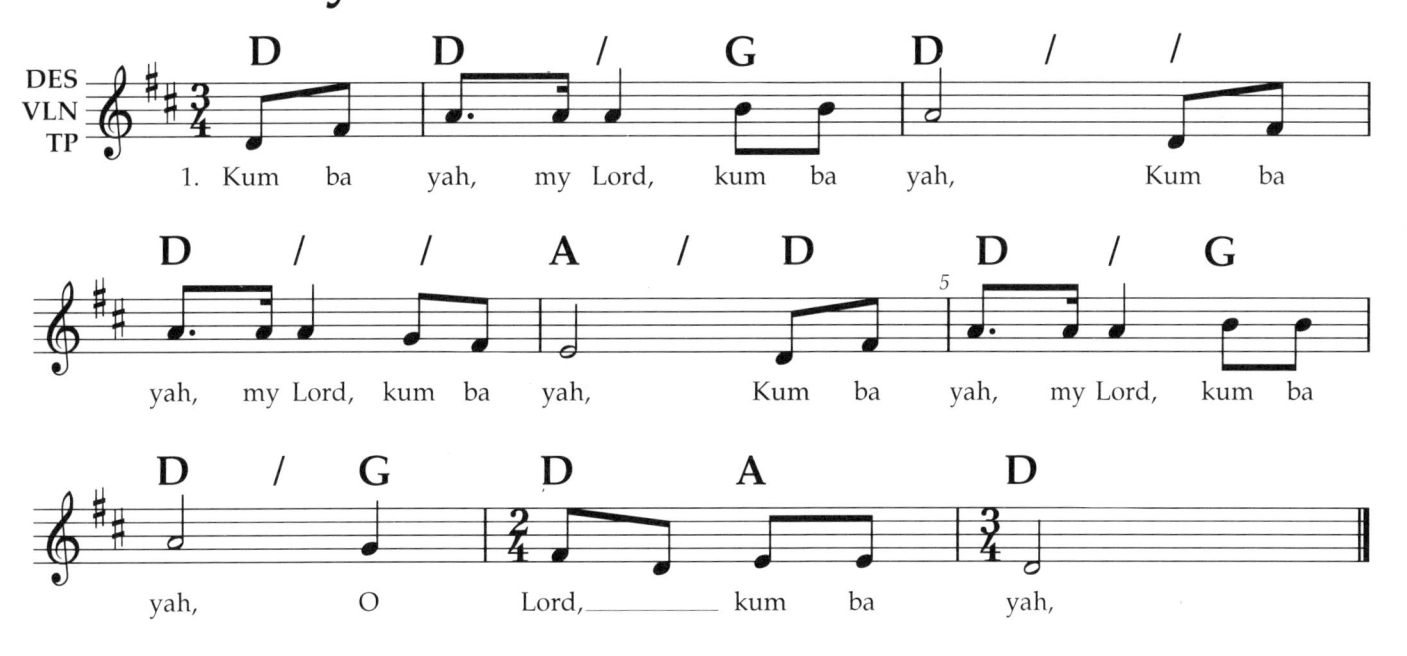

MASTER MELODY

1. Kum ba yah, my Lord, kum ba yah, Kum ba yah, my Lord, kum ba yah, Kum ba yah, my Lord, kum ba yah, O Lord, kum ba yah,

2 Morning has broken *words: Eleanor Farjeon, melody: traditional*

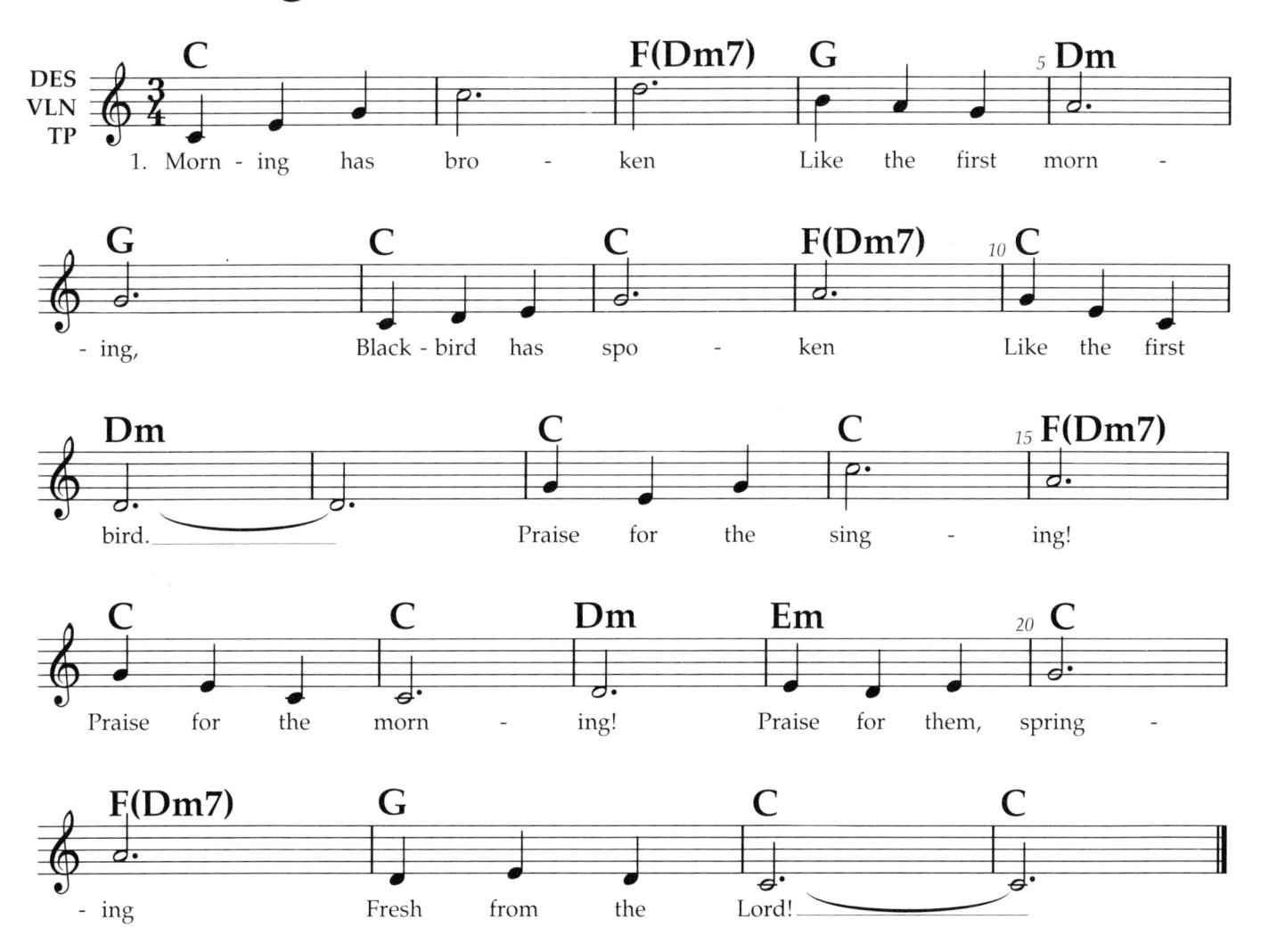

1. Morn-ing has bro-ken Like the first morn-ing, Black-bird has spo-ken Like the first bird. Praise for the sing-ing! Praise for the morn-ing! Praise for them, spring-ing Fresh from the Lord!

© 1990, A & C BLACK (PUBLISHERS) LTD

3 Come and praise the Lord our King
traditional

(Sheet music with chords: C, C, /, Dm, /, C, G7, C *Fine* — Introduction)

A C, C, /, C, /, F, /, C, /
1. Come and praise the Lord our King, Hal-le-lu-jah. Come

C, /, Dm, /, C, G7, C
praise the Lord our King, Hal-le-lu-jah.

B C, C, /, Am, /, F, /, C, /
Christ was born in Beth-le-hem, Hal-le-lu-jah, Son of
Chorus

Em, /, Dm, /, C, G7, C *Last time D.C. al fine*
God and Son of Man, Hal-le-lu-jah.

4 All things which live below the sky
MELODY

words: Edward J. Brailsford, melody: collected and adapted by R. Vaughan Williams

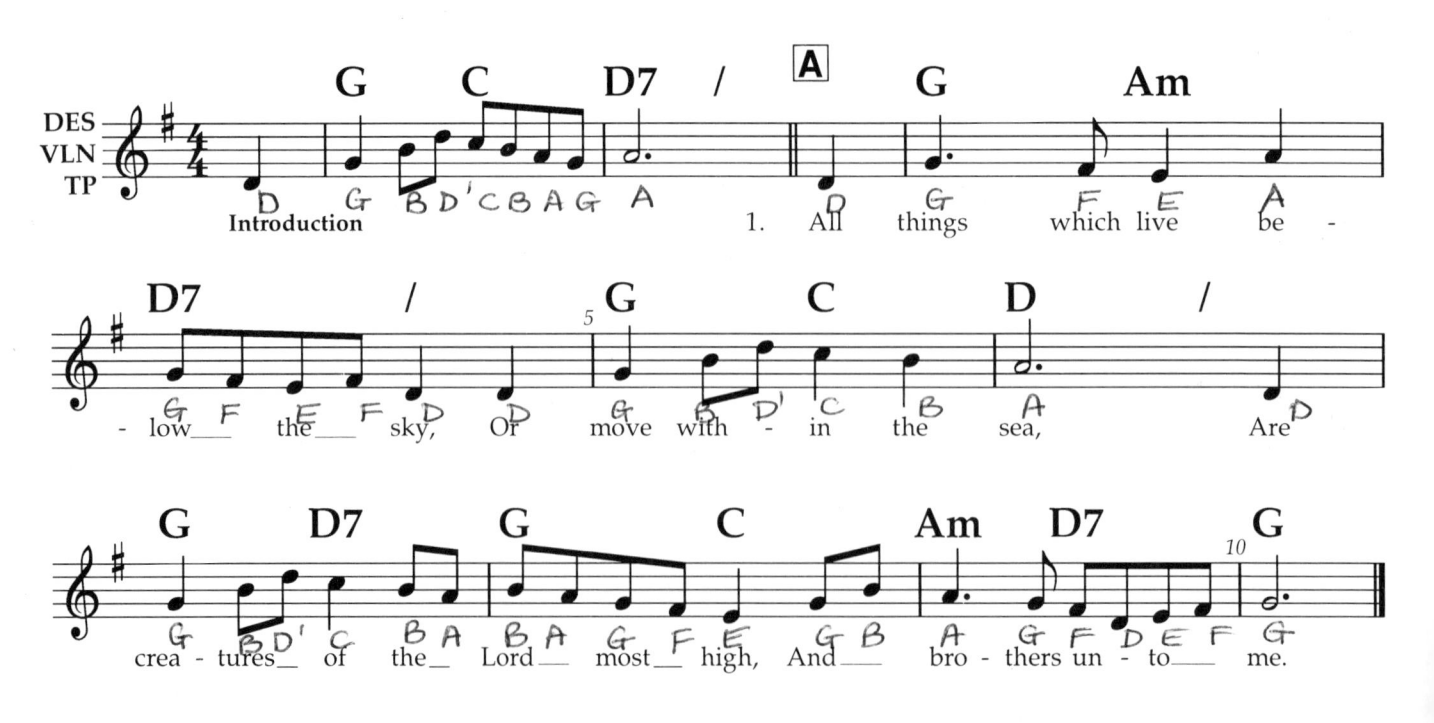

(Introduction: G, C, D7, / — notes: D G B D' C B A G A)

A G, Am, D7, /, G, C, D, /
1. All things which live be-low the sky, Or move with-in the sea, Are
(notes: D G F E A G F E F D D' G B D' C B A D)

G, D7, G, C, Am, D7, G
crea-tures of the Lord most high, And bro-thers un-to me.
(notes: G B D' C B A B A G F E G B A G F D E F G)

5 Every star shall sing a carol *Sydney Carter*

1. Every star shall sing a carol; Every creature, high or low,
Come and praise the King of Heaven By whatever name you know.
God above, Man below, Holy is the name I know.

6 Simple gifts *traditional Shaker song*

Introduction

'Tis the gift to be simple, 'tis the gift to be free, 'Tis the gift to come down where you ought to be, And when we find ourselves in the place just right, 'Twill be in the valley of love and delight. When true simplicity is gained, To bow and to bend we shan't be ashamed; To turn, turn will be our delight, 'Til by turning, turning we come round right.

7 Lord of the harvest
words: Fred Kaan, melody: June Tillman

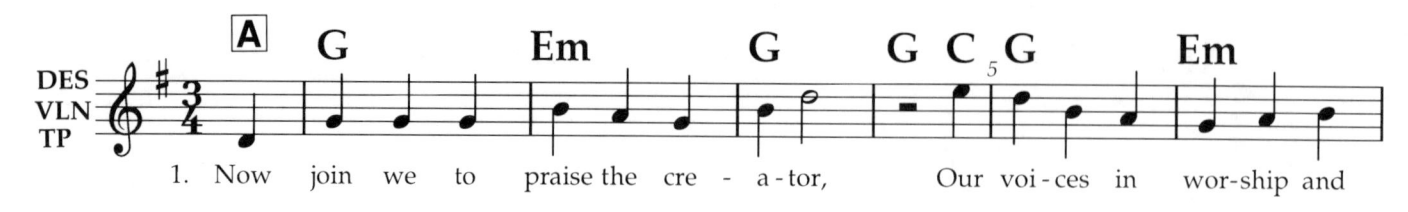

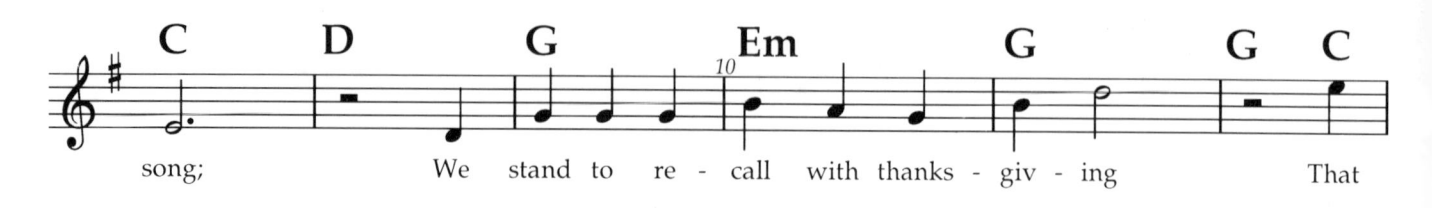

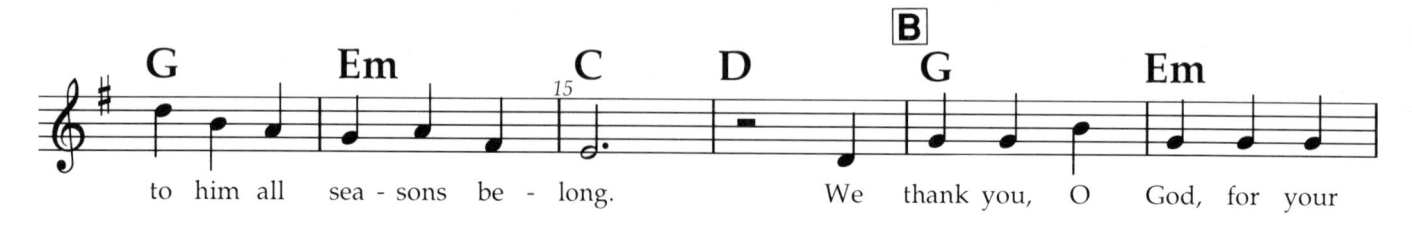

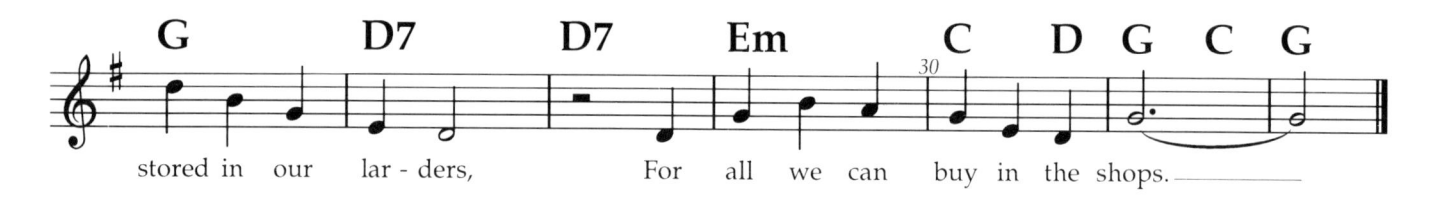

1. Now join we to praise the cre-a-tor, Our voi-ces in wor-ship and song; We stand to re-call with thanks-giv-ing That to him all sea-sons be-long. We thank you, O God, for your good-ness, For the joy and a-bun-dance of crops, For food that is stored in our lar-ders, For all we can buy in the shops.

8 The vine and the fig tree
traditional

Introduction

And eve-ry-one be-neath the vine and fig tree, Shall live in peace and have no fear. And eve-ry-

[C] -one beneath the vine and fig tree, Shall live in

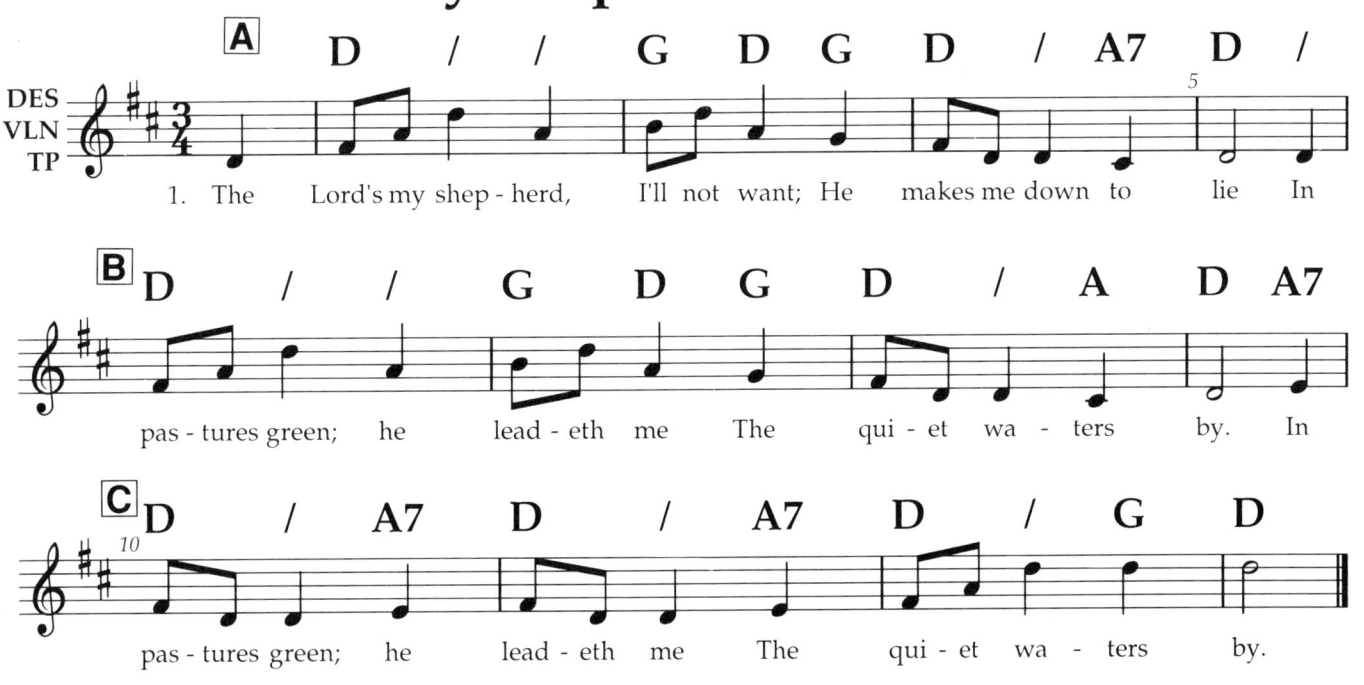

[D] peace and have no fear. *Fine*

[E] And into plough-shares turn their swords,

[F] Nations shall learn war no more.

[G] And into plough-shares turn their swords,

[H] Nations shall learn war no more. And eve-ry- *Repeat from A to fine*

9 The Lord's my shepherd
words: W. Whittingham, melody: J. L. MacBeth Bain

[A] 1. The Lord's my shep-herd, I'll not want; He makes me down to lie In

[B] pas-tures green; he lead-eth me The qui-et wa-ters by. In

[C] pas-tures green; he lead-eth me The qui-et wa-ters by.

10 Lord of the ocean
words: David Harding, melody: (Skye Boat Song) traditional

A | G | Em | Am | D7 | G | C | G / *Fine*

1. Lord of the o-cean so vast and so free, Lord of the run-ning tide,
   Lord of all po-wer and my-ste-ry, hum-ble our nar-row pride.

B | Em / | Am / | Em C | Em /

Yours is the love! Yours is the power! Yours is the pur-pose wide!

Em / | Am / | Em C | Em D7 *D. C. al fine*

Ours is your love, Ours is your power, Ours is your pur-pose wide.

11 Bread and fishes
Alan Bell

A + **D** | D | G | A7 | D

1. As I was a-walk-ing in the spring-time one day, I
   have bread and fish-es and a jug of red wine To

(Bm) | Em | A7 | D | D *Fine*

met with some tra-vellers in an old coun-try lane. One was an
share on our jour-ney with all of man-kind.

G | A7 | D | (Bm) | Em

old man, the se-cond a maid, The third was a young man who

C | A7 | D | G | D | G

smiled as he said: With the wind in the wil-lows and the birds in the

D | G | D | Em | A7 *D. S. al fine*

sky; And the bright sun to warm us wher-e-ver we lie, We

12 Sing hosanna *traditional*

Introduction

1. Give me joy in my heart, keep me prais-ing— Give me joy in my heart, I pray; Give me joy in my heart, Keep me prais-ing,— Keep me prais-ing till the break of day:

Chorus

Sing Ho-san-na! Sing Ho-san-na! Sing Ho-san-na to the King of Kings! Sing Ho-san-na! Sing Ho-san-na! Sing Ho-san-na to the King.

13 The day thou gavest *words: John Ellerton, melody: Clement C. Scholefield*

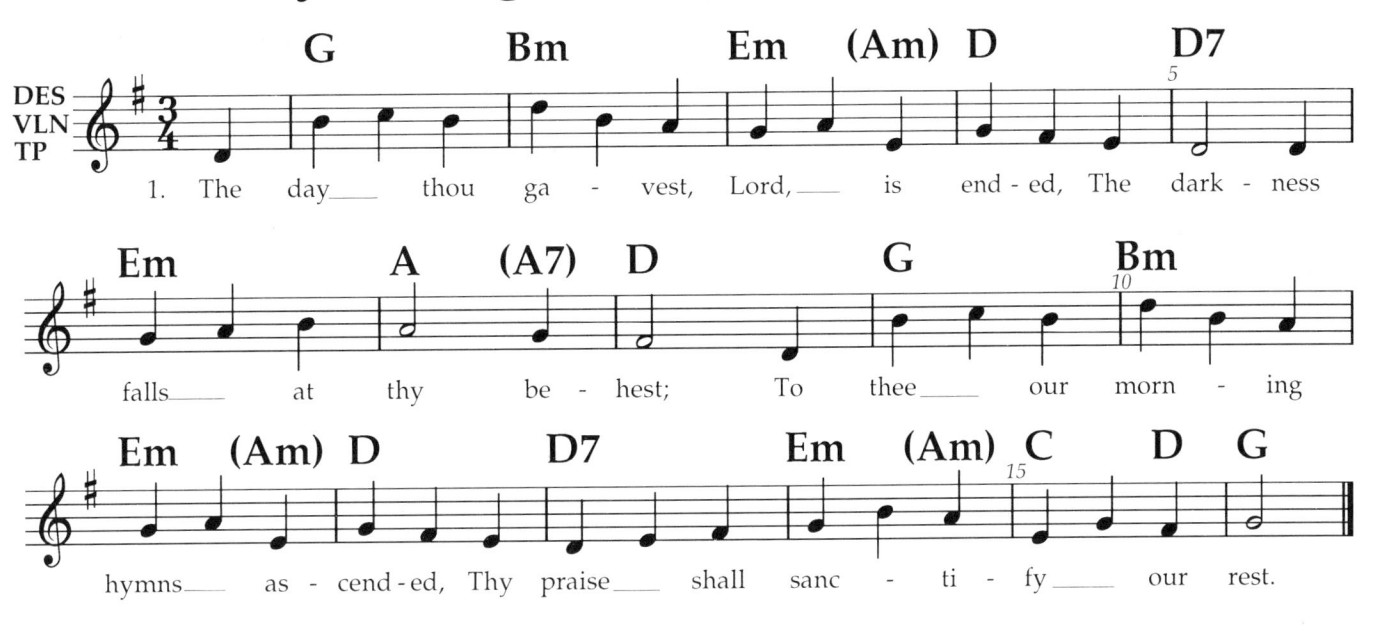

1. The day— thou ga-vest, Lord,— is end-ed, The dark-ness falls— at thy be-hest; To thee— our morn-ing hymns— as-cend-ed, Thy praise— shall sanc-ti-fy— our rest.

14 Make me a channel of your peace
Sebastian Temple

Introduction

1. Make me a chan-nel of your peace. ___ Where there is hat-red, let me bring your love; ___ Where there is in-ju-ry, your par-don, Lord; ___ And where there's doubt, true faith in you. ___ O Mas-ter, grant that I may ne-ver seek ___ So much to be con-soled as to con-sole, ___ To be un-der-stood as to un-der-stand: ___ To be loved, as to love with all my soul. ___

Repeat A

The following copyright owners have kindly granted their permission for the reprinting of words and music:

Franciscan Communications for the words and melody of *14 Make me a channel of your peace* by Sebastian Temple.

David Harding for the words of *10 Lord of the ocean*.

David Higham Associates for the words of *2 Morning has broken* by Eleanor Farjeon.

Maypole Music Ltd for the words and melody of *11 Bread and fishes* by Alan Bell.

Oxford University Press for the melody of *4 All things which live below the sky* collected and adapted by R. Vaughan Williams.

Stainer & Bell Ltd and Hope Publishing Co for the words of *7 Lord of the harvest* by Fred Kaan.

Stainer & Bell Ltd and Galaxy Music Corp for the words and melody of *5 Every star shall sing a carol* by Sydney Carter, and the melody of *7 Lord of the harvest*, adapted from a Scottish tune by June Tillman.

1 Kum ba yah

PART 1 ADVANCED REC/TP/VLN

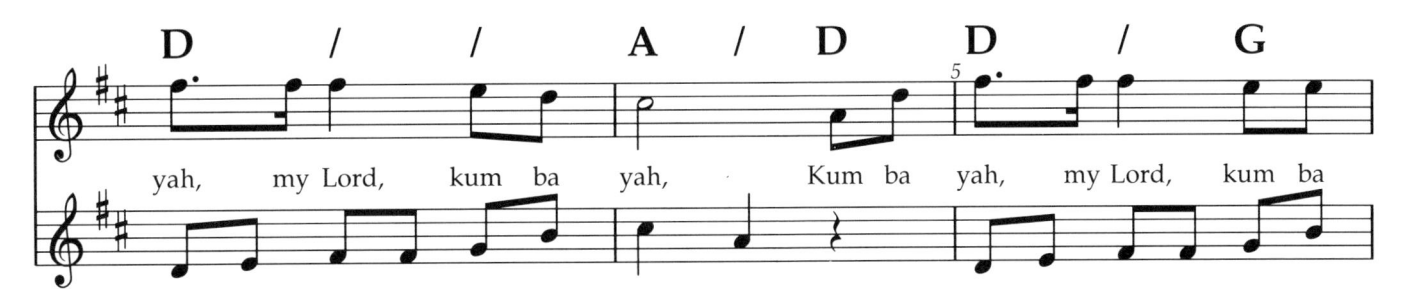

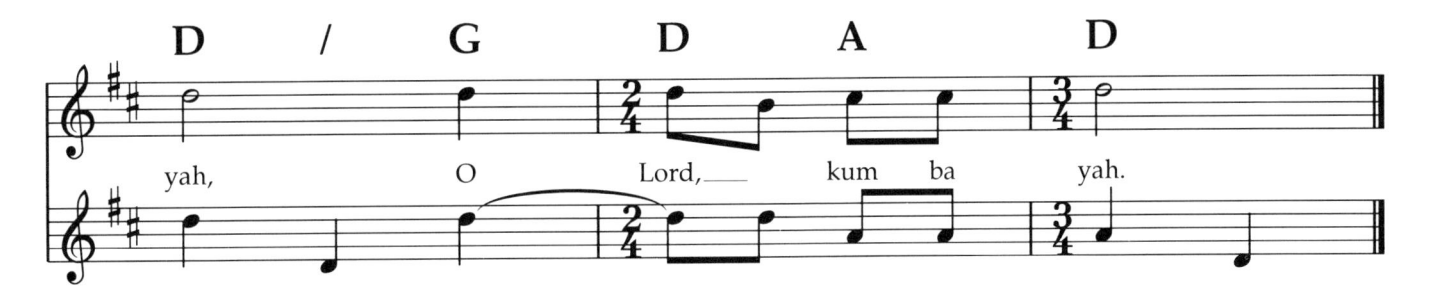

Kum ba yah, my Lord, kum ba yah, Kum ba yah, my Lord, kum ba yah, Kum ba yah, my Lord, kum ba yah, O Lord, kum ba yah.

2 Morning has broken

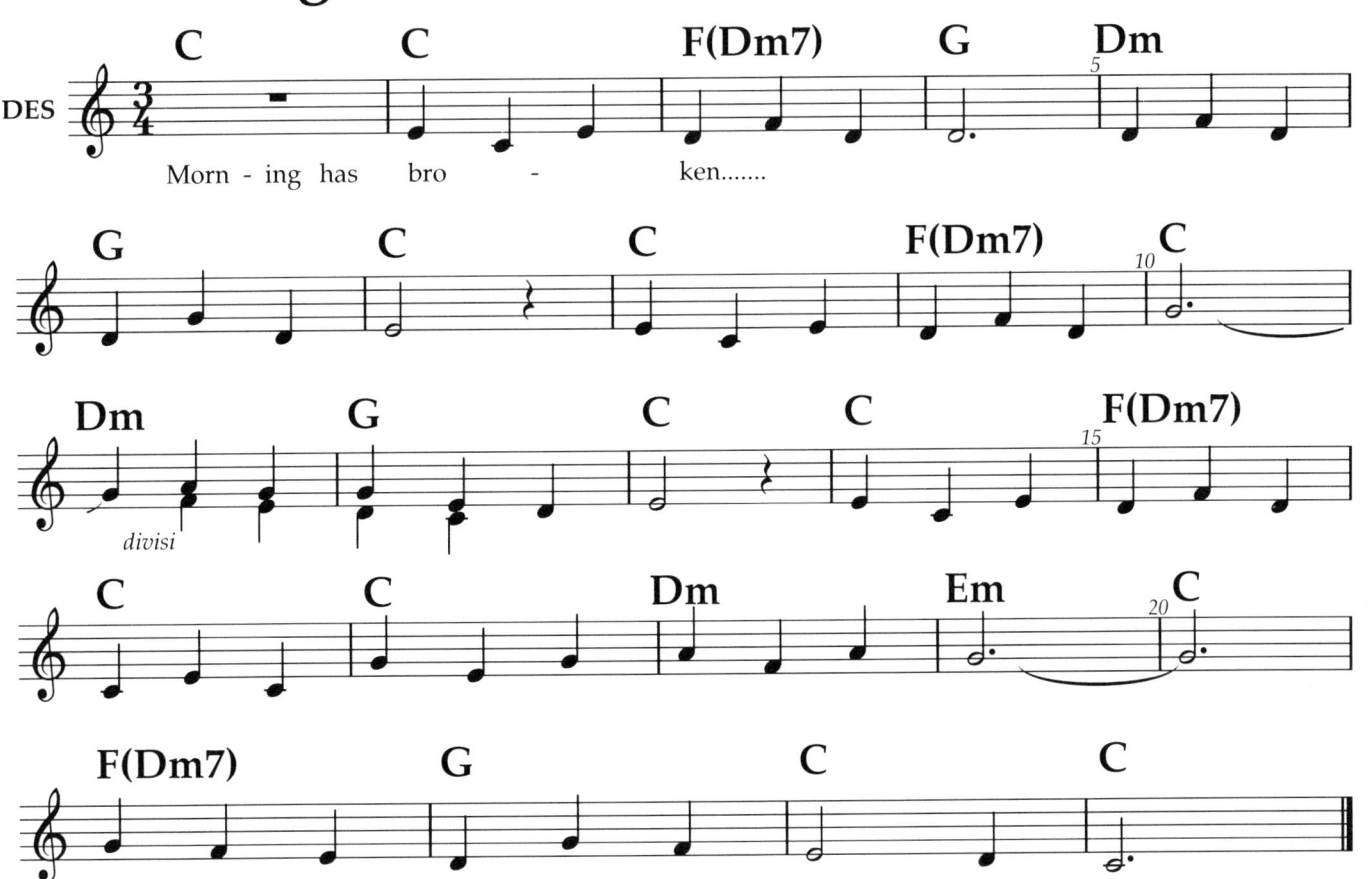

Morn - ing has bro - ken.......

divisi

© 1990, A & C BLACK (PUBLISHERS) LTD

3 Come and praise the Lord our King

4 All things which live below the sky

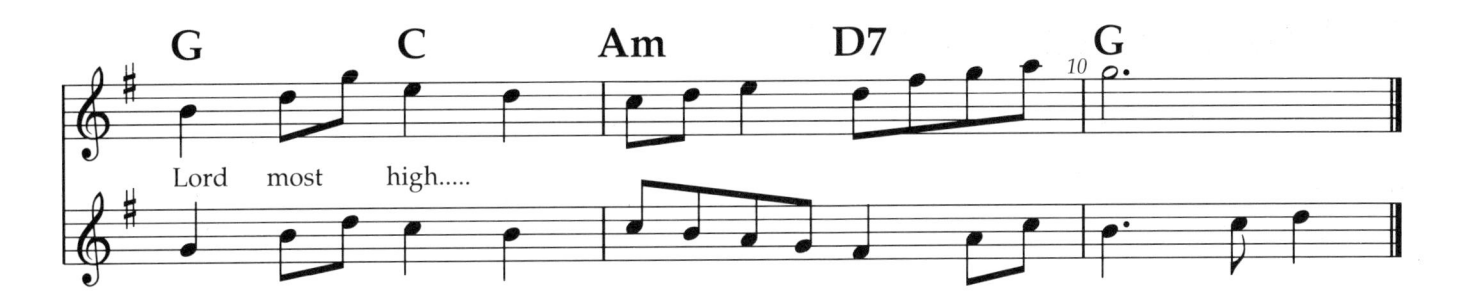

5 Every star shall sing a carol

6 Simple gifts

7 Lord of the harvest

cre - a - tor ...

song ...

thanks - giv - ing ...

sea - sons be - long ...

good - ness ...

a - bundance of crops ...

8 The vine and the fig tree

Introduction

9 The Lord's my shepherd

10 Lord of the ocean

11 Bread and fishes

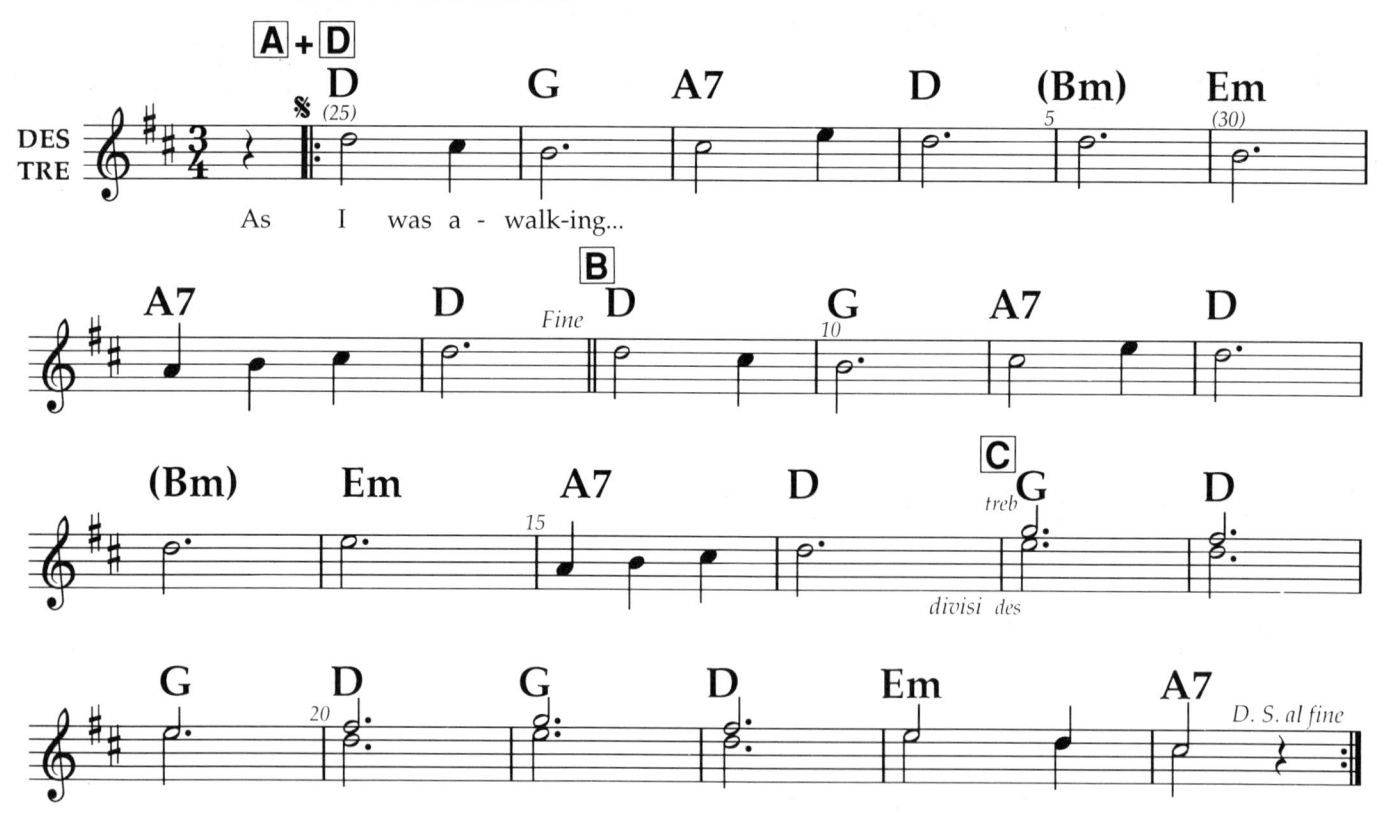

As I was a-walking...

12 Sing Hosanna

Introduction   Give me joy in my heart, keep me praising...

13 The day thou gavest

14 Make me a channel of your peace

MASTER

1 Kum ba yah

PART 1 ADVANCED
REC/TP/VLN

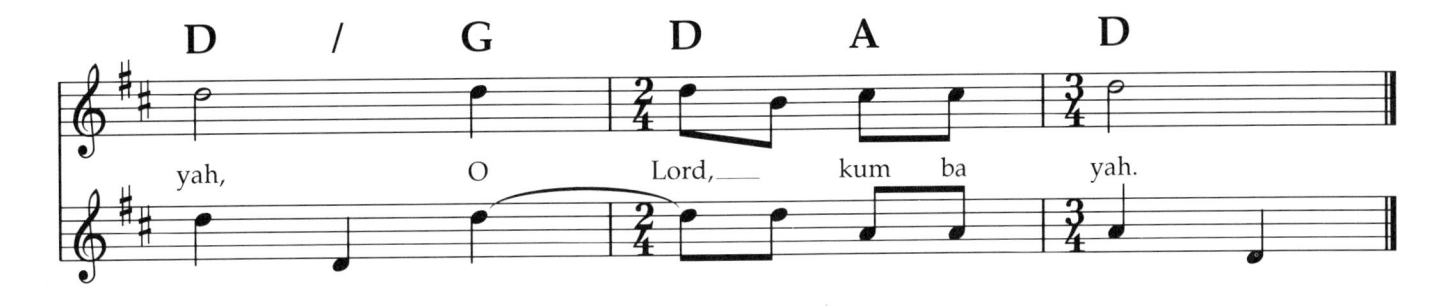

3 Come and praise the Lord our King

4 All things which live below the sky

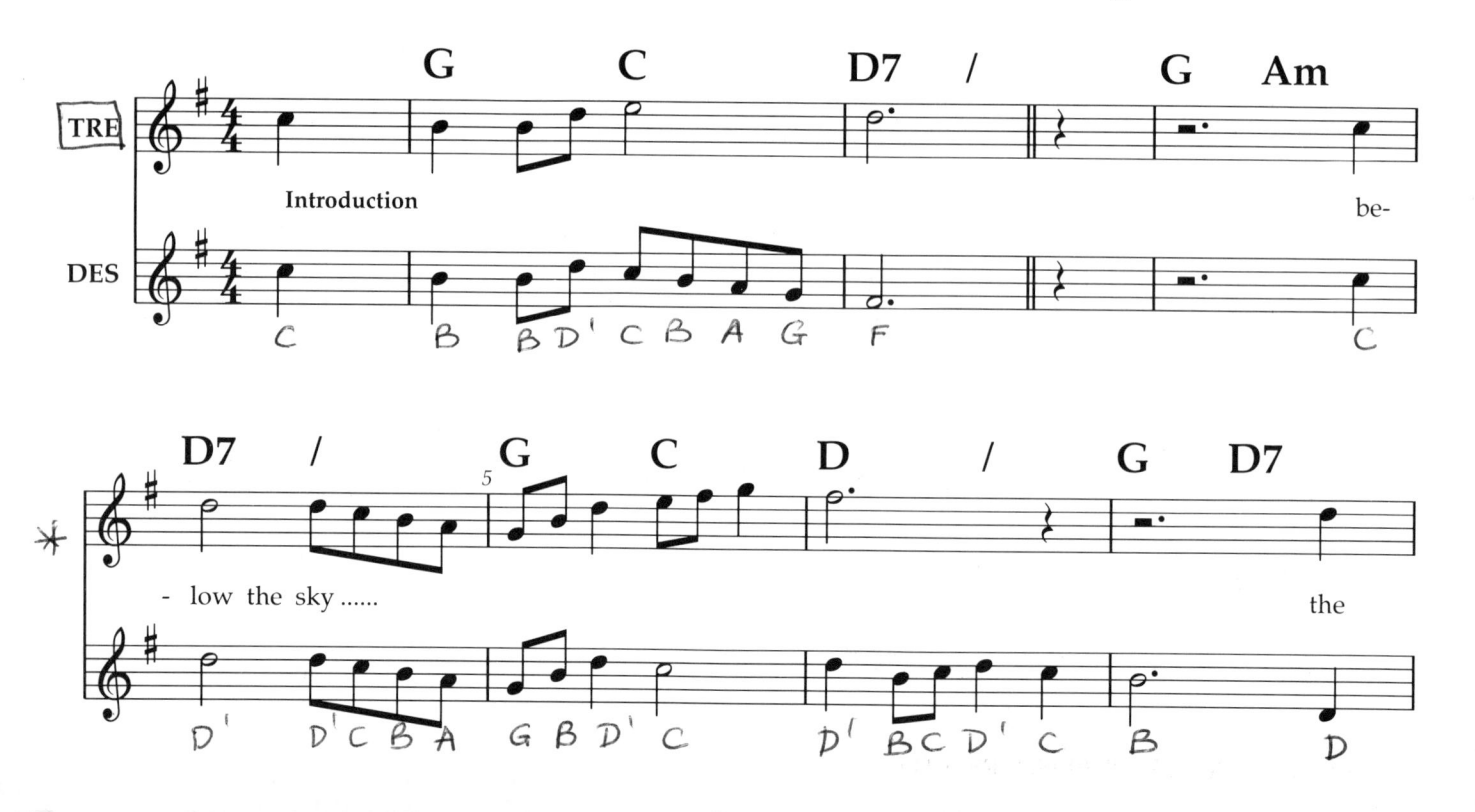

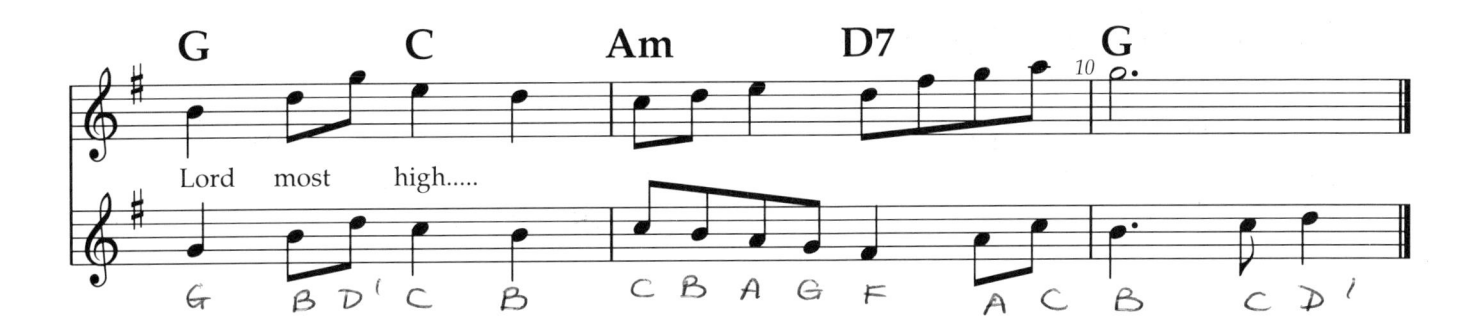

5 Every star shall sing a carol

6 Simple gifts

7 Lord of the harvest

cre - a - tor ...
song ...
thanks - giv - ing ...
sea - sons be - long ...
good - ness ...
a - bundance of crops ...

8 The vine and the fig tree

Introduction

9 The Lord's my shepherd

10 Lord of the ocean

11 Bread and fishes

12 Sing Hosanna

joy in my heart, keep me praising...

(des/tre)

13 The day thou gavest

14 Make me a channel of your peace

1 Kum ba yah

PART 2 REC

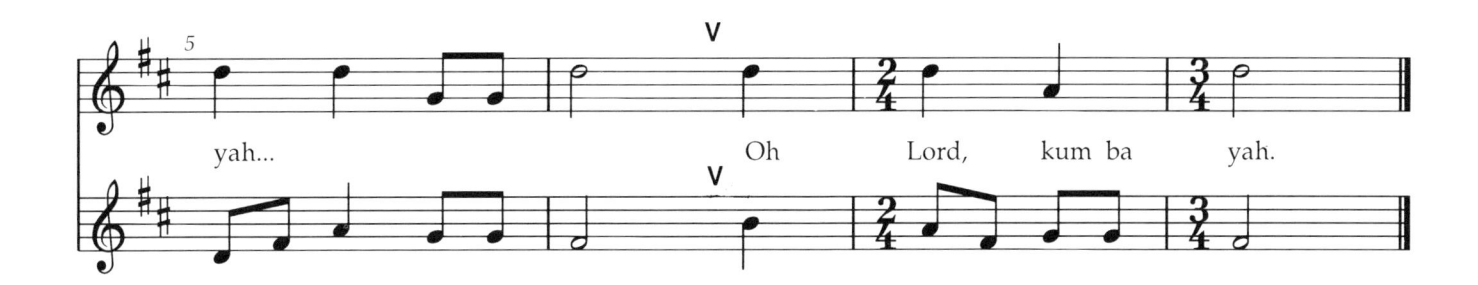

Kum ba yah.... Kum ba yah.... Kum ba yah... Oh Lord, kum ba yah.

2 Morning has broken

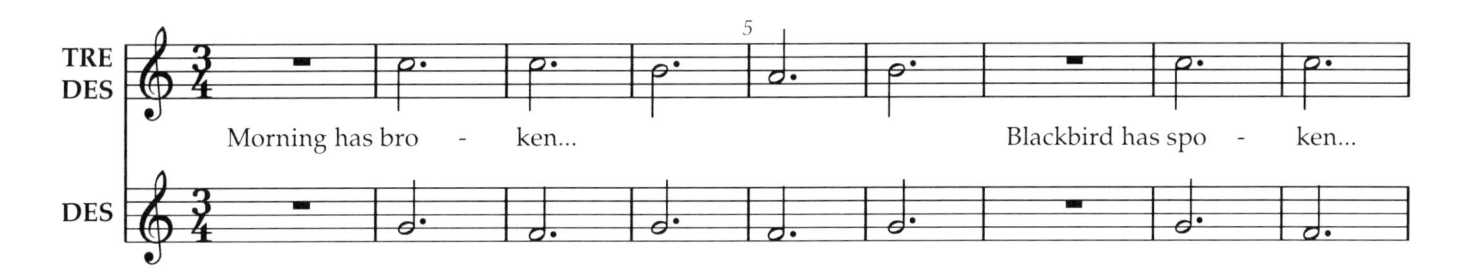

Morning has bro - ken... Blackbird has spo - ken...

Praise for the sing - ing...

Praise for them, spring - ing...

divisi

© 1990, A & C BLACK (PUBLISHERS) LTD.

3 Come and praise the Lord our King

4 All things which live below the sky

5 Every star shall sing a carol

1. Eve - ry star

6 Simple gifts

Introduction   'Tis the gift......

When true......

7 Lord of the harvest

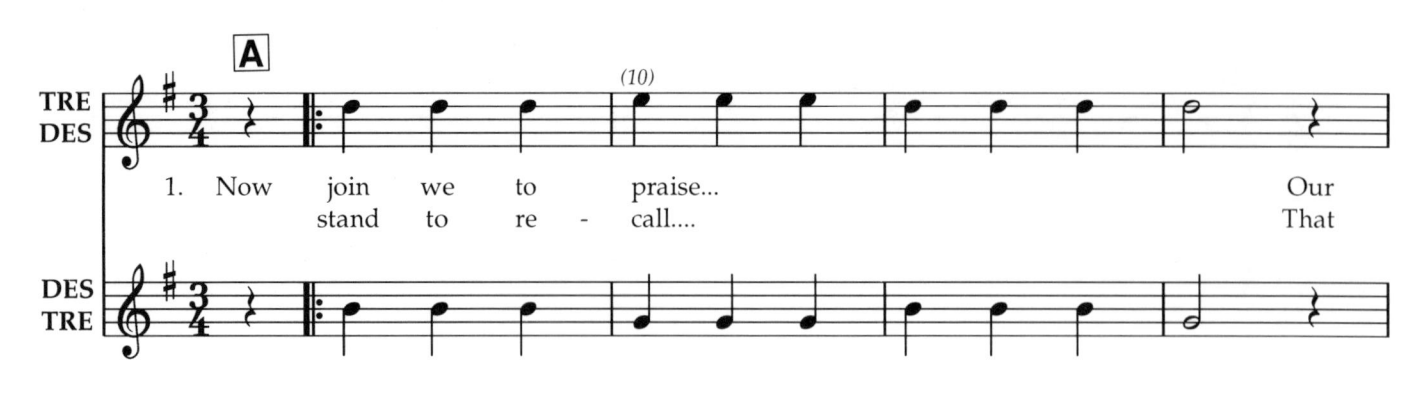

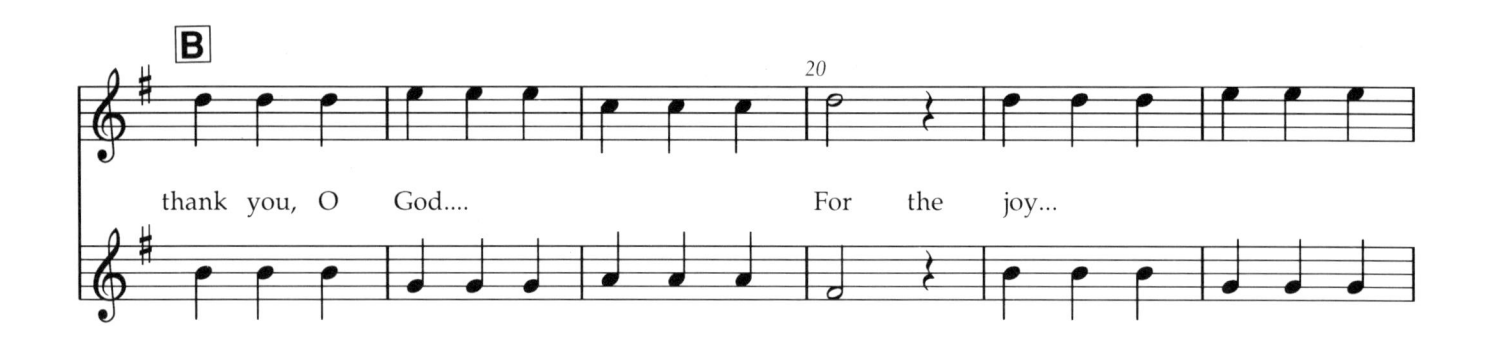

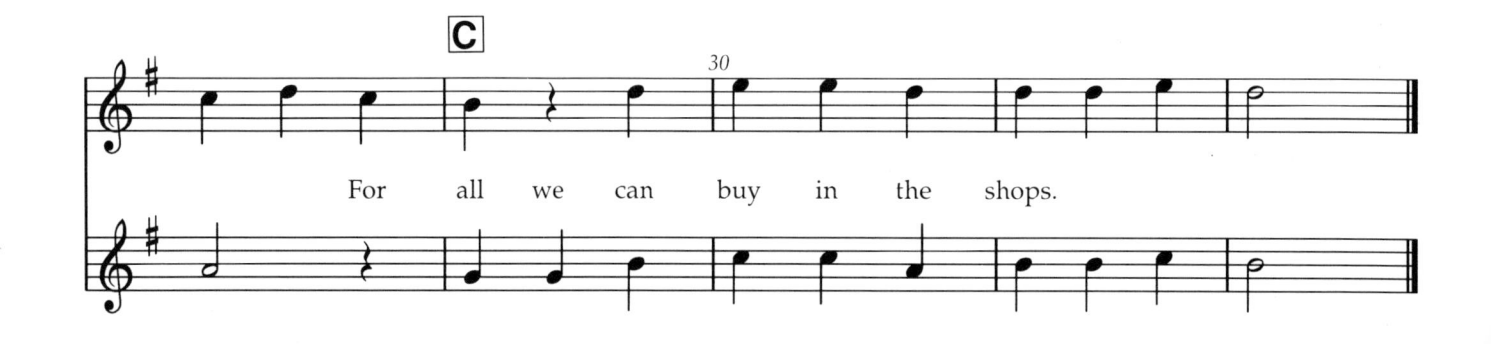

1. Now join we to praise... Our voices... We
   stand to re-call.... That to him... We

thank you, O God.... For the joy...

For food...

For all we can buy in the shops.

8 The vine and the fig tree

9 The Lord's my shepherd

10 Lord of the ocean

1. Lord of the o-cean so...

Yours is the love...

play twice then D. C. al fine

11 Bread and fishes

1. As I was a-walking...
have bread and fishes...

One was an old man..... With the

wind in the willows... We

12 Sing Hosanna

Introduction

1. Give me joy...

Sing... Sing... Sing... King of Kings Sing... Sing... Sing... King.

chorus

divisi

13 The day thou gavest

1. The day___ thou ga-vest...

To thee___ our morn-ing hymns...

14 Make me a channel of your peace

Make me a channel of your peace.

Where there is injury, your pardon, Lord; And where there's doubt... O

Master, grant that I... So much to be con- soled... To be understood... To be loved...

1 Kum ba yah

PART 2 REC

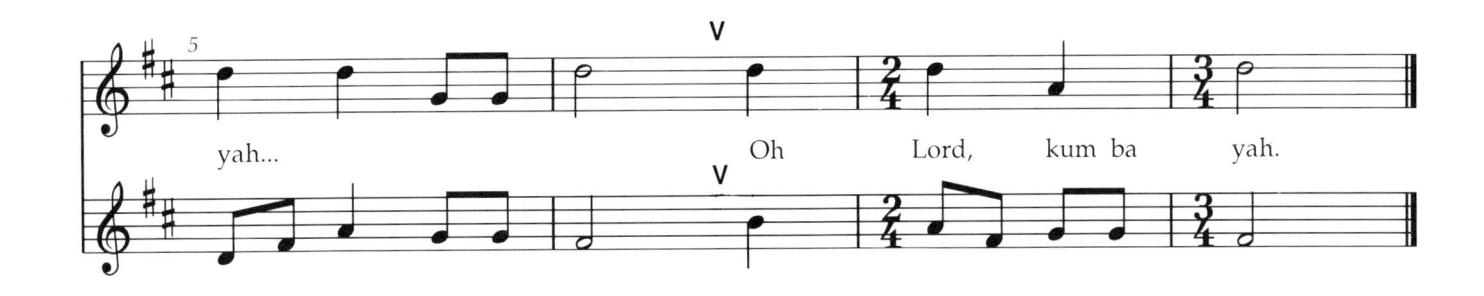

2 Morning has broken

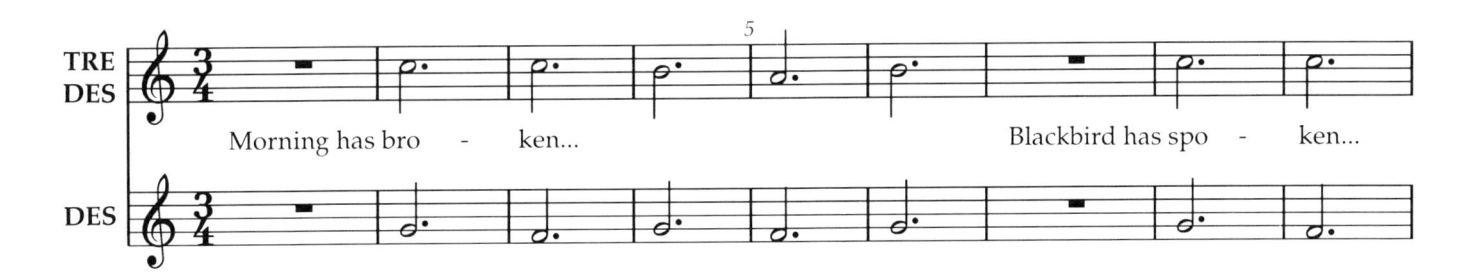

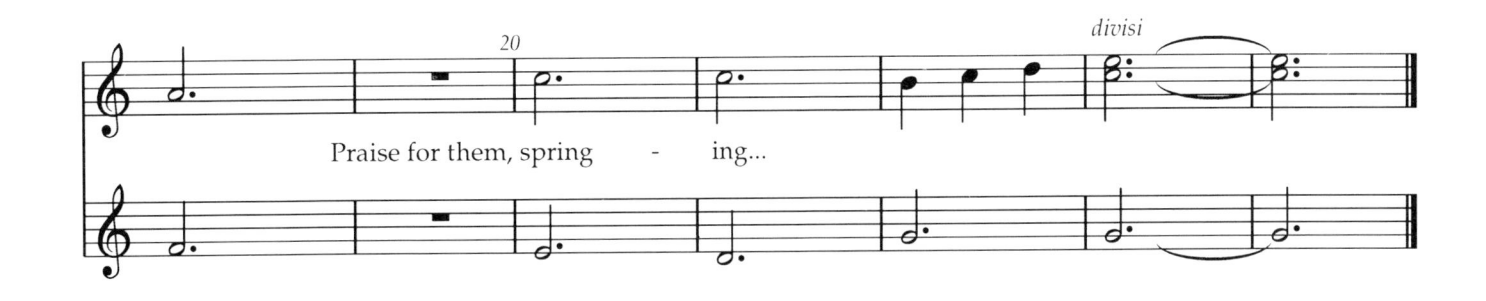

© 1990, A & C BLACK (PUBLISHERS) LTD.

3 Come and praise the Lord our King

4 All things which live below the sky

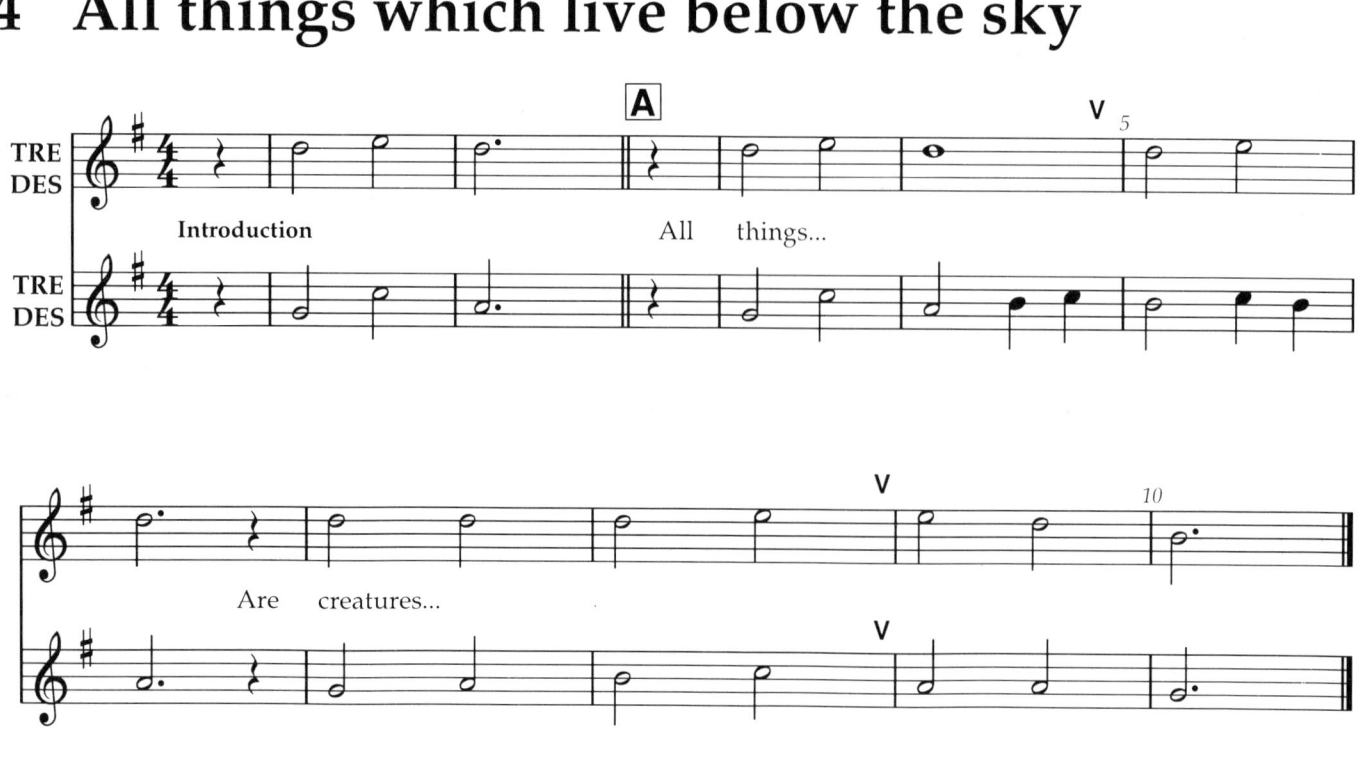

5 Every star shall sing a carol

1. Eve-ry star

6 Simple gifts

Introduction — 'Tis the gift.......

When true......

7 Lord of the harvest

1. Now join we to praise... Our
   stand to re-call.... That

   voi-ces... We
   to him... We

   thank you, O God.... For the joy...

   For food...

   For all we can buy in the shops.

8 The vine and the fig tree

Intro And every-one...

9 The Lord's my shepherd

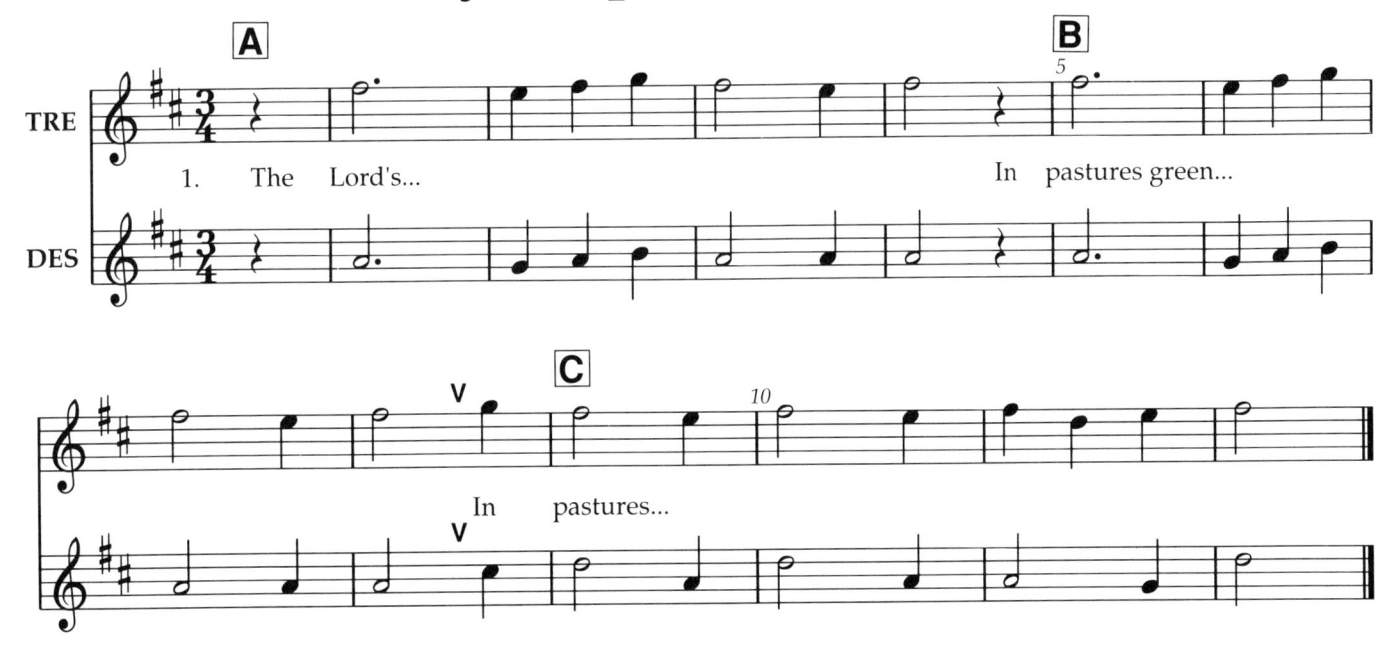

1. The Lord's...

In pastures green...

In pastures...

10 Lord of the ocean

1. Lord of the o-cean so...

Yours is the love...

play twice then D. C. al fine

11 Bread and fishes

1. As I was a-walking...
have bread and fishes...

One was an old man..... With the

wind in the willows... We

D. S. al fine

12 Sing Hosanna

Introduction

1. Give me joy...

Sing... Sing... Sing... King of Kings Sing... Sing... Sing... King.

chorus

divisi

13 The day thou gavest

1. The day___ thou ga-vest...

To thee___ our morn-ing hymns...

14 Make me a channel of your peace

Make me a channel of your peace.

Where there is in-ju-ry, your par-don, Lord; And where there's doubt... O Master, grant that I... So much to be con- -soled... To be un-der-stood... To be loved...

1 Kum ba yah

PART 2 REC

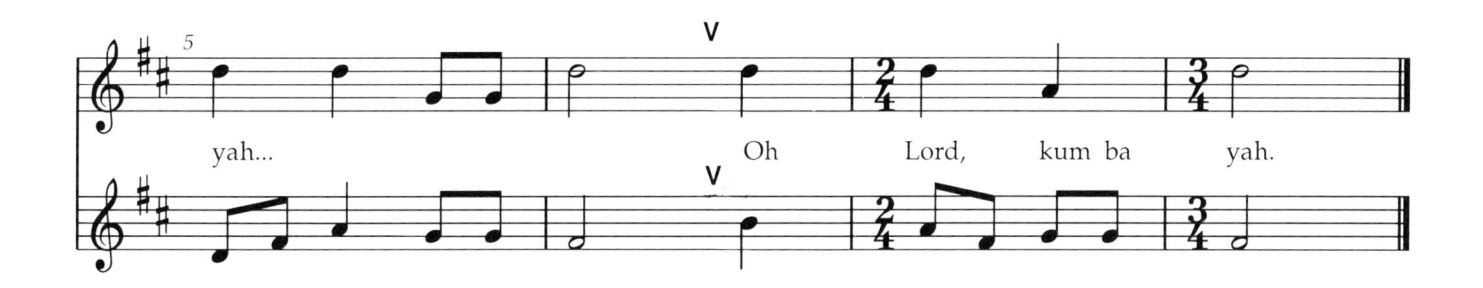

Kum ba yah.... Kum ba yah.... Kum ba yah... Oh Lord, kum ba yah.

2 Morning has broken

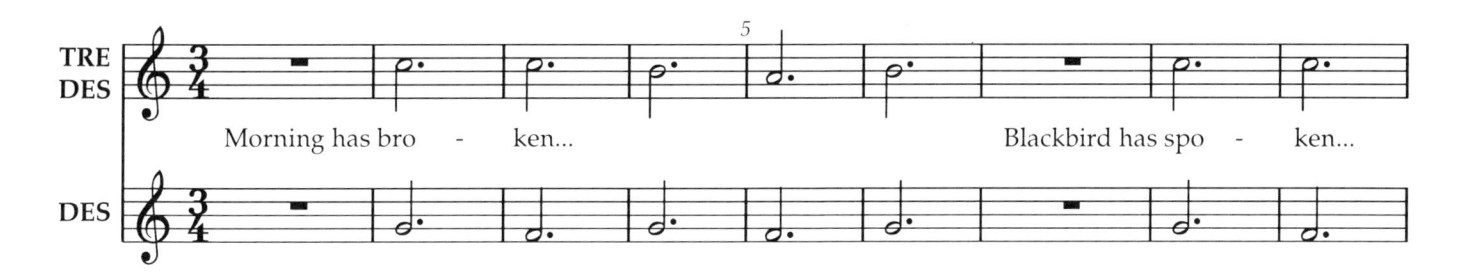

Morning has bro - ken... Blackbird has spo - ken...

Praise for the sing - ing...

divisi

Praise for them, spring - ing...

© 1990, A & C Black (Publishers) Ltd.

3 Come and praise the Lord our King

4 All things which live below the sky

5 Every star shall sing a carol

1. Eve - ry star

6 Simple gifts

Introduction   'Tis the gift.......

When true......

7 Lord of the harvest

1. Now join we to praise... Our voices... We
   stand to recall... That to him... We

thank you, O God.... For the joy...

For food...

For all we can buy in the shops.

8 The vine and the fig tree

Intro And every-one...

9 The Lord's my shepherd

1. The Lord's...   In pastures green...

In pastures...

10 Lord of the ocean

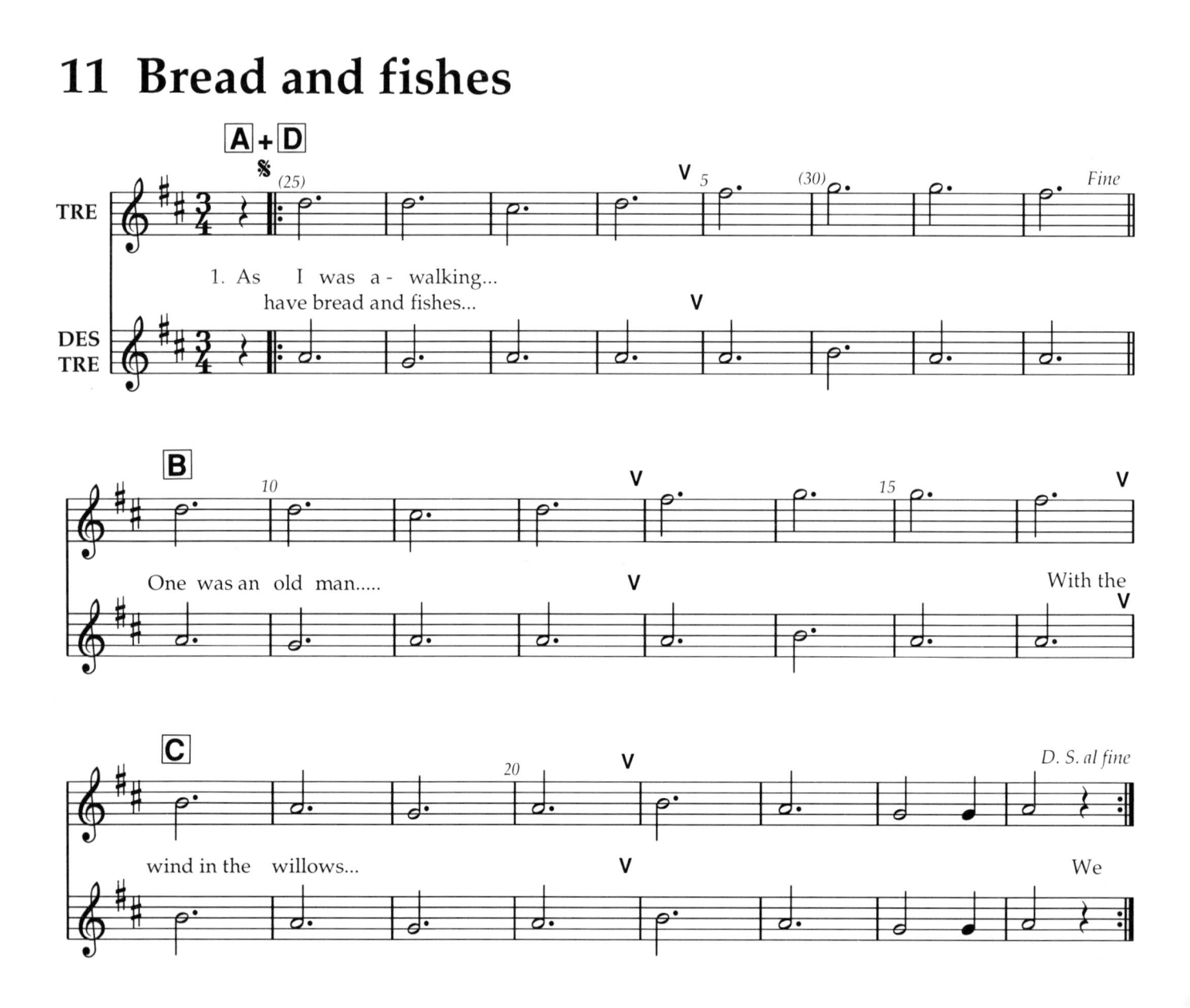

1. Lord of the o-cean so...

Yours is the love...

play twice then D.C. al fine

11 Bread and fishes

1. As I was a-walking...
have bread and fishes...

One was an old man..... With the

wind in the willows... We

12 Sing Hosanna

Introduction

1. Give me joy...

Sing... Sing... Sing... King of Kings Sing... Sing... Sing... King.

chorus   *divisi*

13 The day thou gavest

1. The day___ thou ga - vest...

To thee___ our morn - ing hymns...

14 Make me a channel of your peace

Make me a channel of your peace.

Where there is in-ju-ry, your par-don,

Lord; And where there's doubt... O

Master, grant that I... So much to be con-

- soled... To be un-der-stood...

To be loved...

1 Kum ba yah

PART 3 VLN

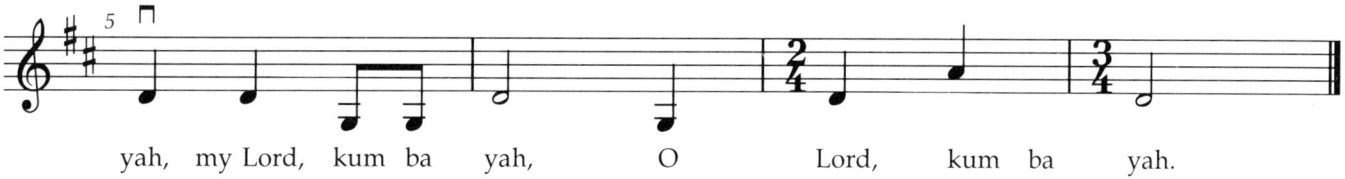

Kum ba yah, my Lord, kum ba yah, Kum ba yah, my Lord, kum ba yah, Kum ba yah, my Lord, kum ba yah, O Lord, kum ba yah.

2 Morning has broken

Morning has bro - ken...

Black bird has spo - ken...

Praise for the sing - ing...

Praise for them, spring - ing...

divisi

©1990, A & C BLACK (PUBLISHERS) LTD.

3 Come and praise the Lord our King

4 All things which live below the sky

5 Every star shall sing a carol

Eve - ry star shall sing a ca - rol...

6 Simple gifts

Introduction   'Tis the gift to be simple.....

7 Lord of the harvest

Now join we to praise the cre - a - tor...

8 The vine and the fig tree

Introduction And every-one be-neath the vine and fig tree...

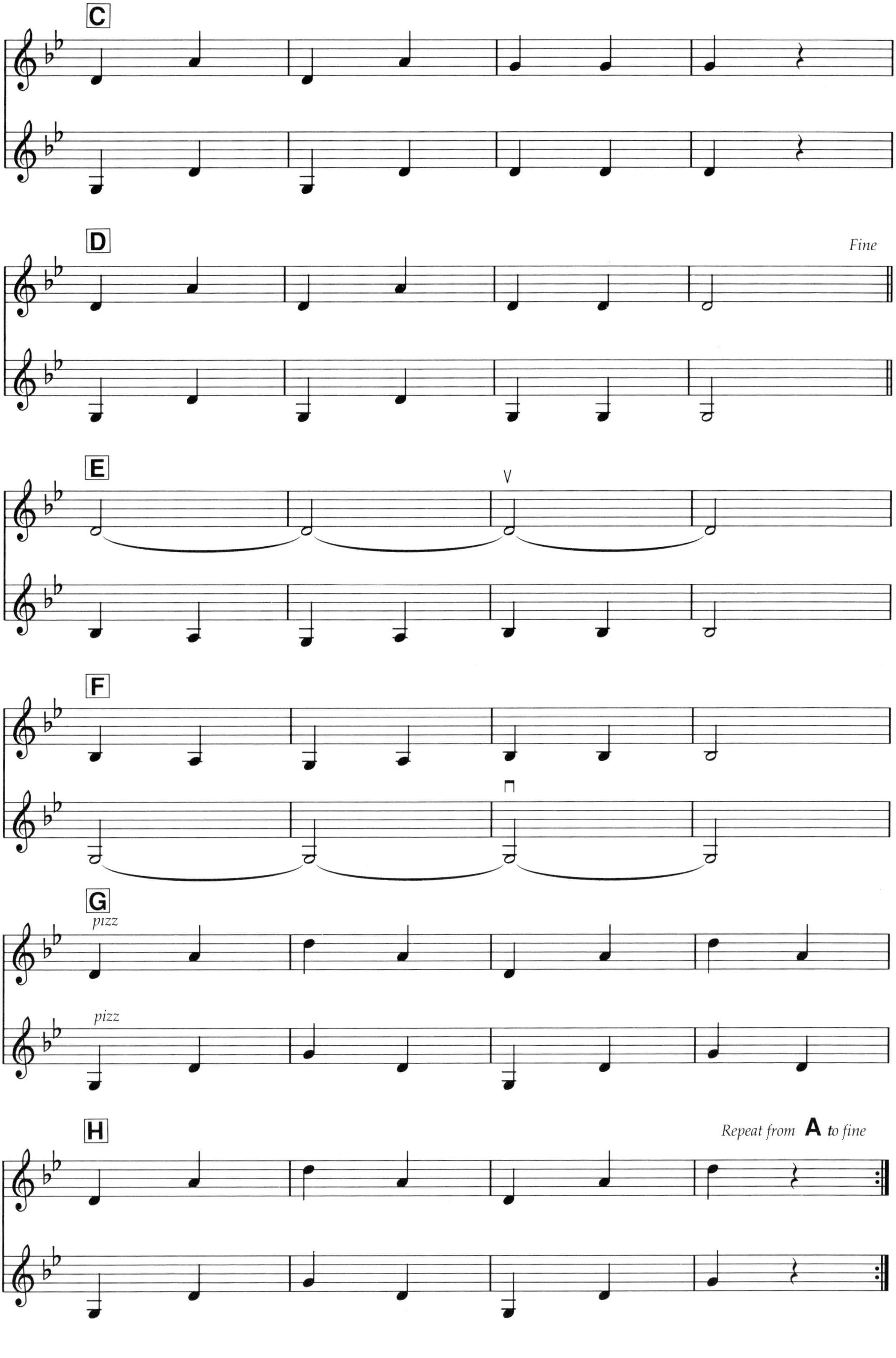
C
D
Fine
E
F
G
pizz
pizz
H
Repeat from A to fine

9 The Lord's my shepherd

The Lord's my shep - herd...
past - tures green he...
In
In

pas - tures green...

10 Lord of the ocean

Fine

play twice then D. C. al fine

11 Bread and fishes

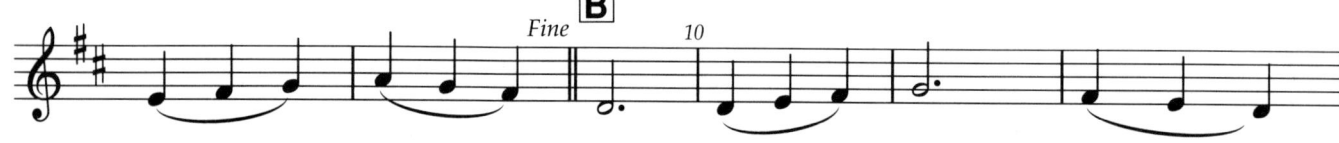

As I was a walking in the springtime......

Fine

12 Sing Hosanna

13 The day thou gavest

14 Make me a channel of your peace

Introduction   Make me a channel of your peace.

1 Kum ba yah

PART 3 VLN

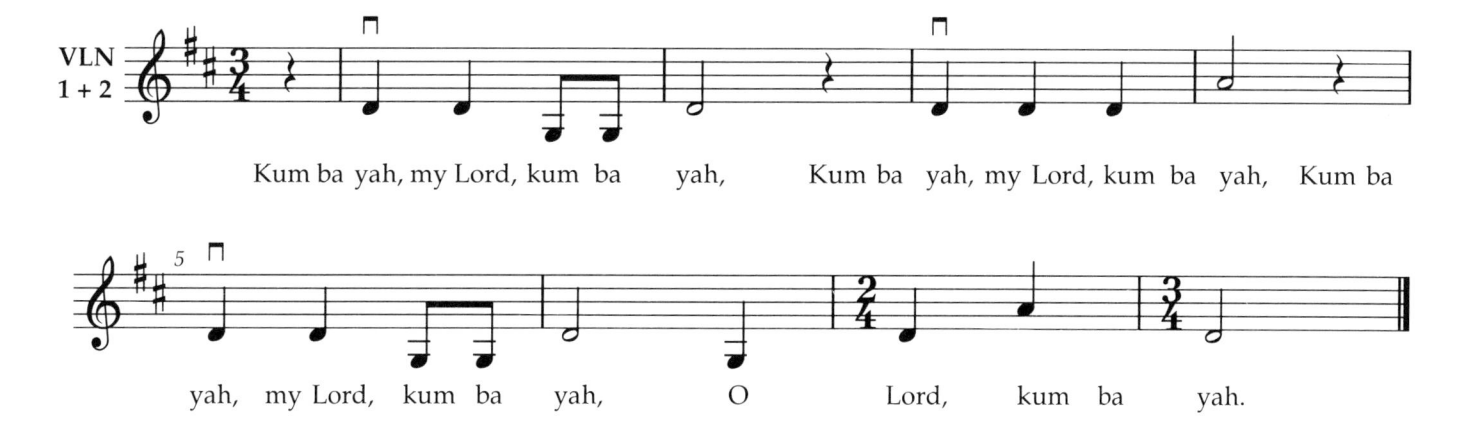

Kum ba yah, my Lord, kum ba yah, Kum ba yah, my Lord, kum ba yah, Kum ba yah, my Lord, kum ba yah, O Lord, kum ba yah.

2 Morning has broken

Morning has bro - ken...

Black bird has spo - ken...

Praise for the sing - ing...

Praise for them, spring - ing...

divisi

©1990, A & C BLACK (PUBLISHERS) LTD.

3 Come and praise the Lord our King

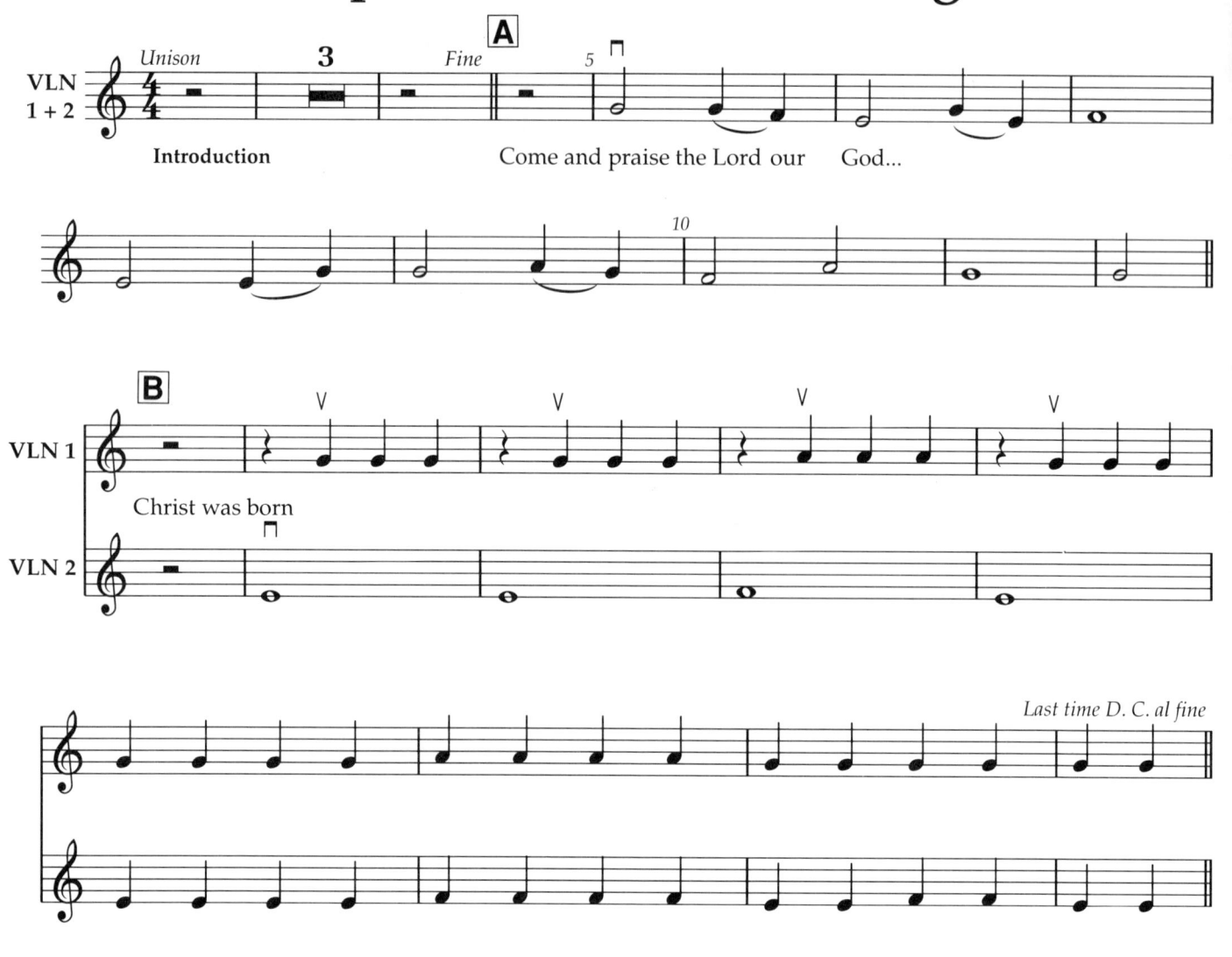

4 All things which live below the sky

5 Every star shall sing a carol

Eve - ry star shall sing a ca - rol...

6 Simple gifts

Introduction   'Tis the gift to be simple.....

7 Lord of the harvest

Now join we to praise the cre - a - tor...

8 The vine and the fig tree

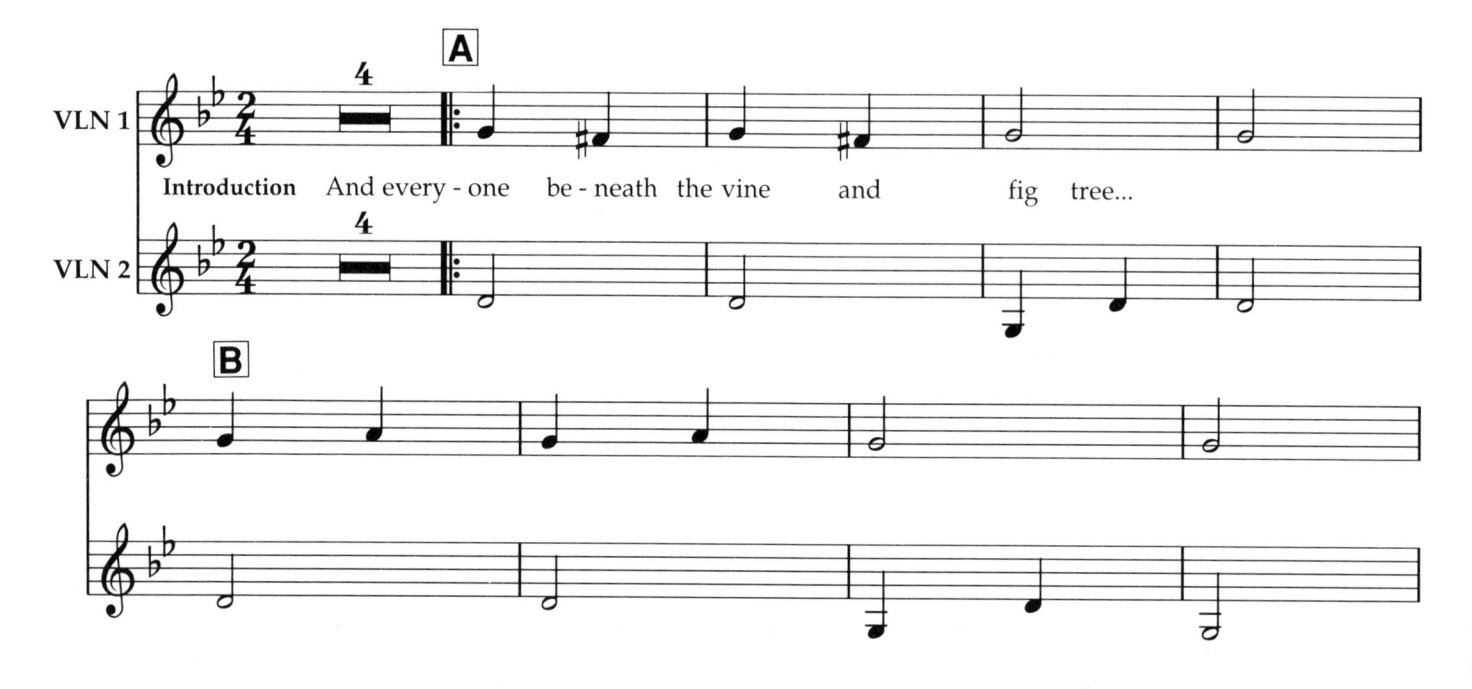

Introduction And every - one be - neath the vine and fig tree...

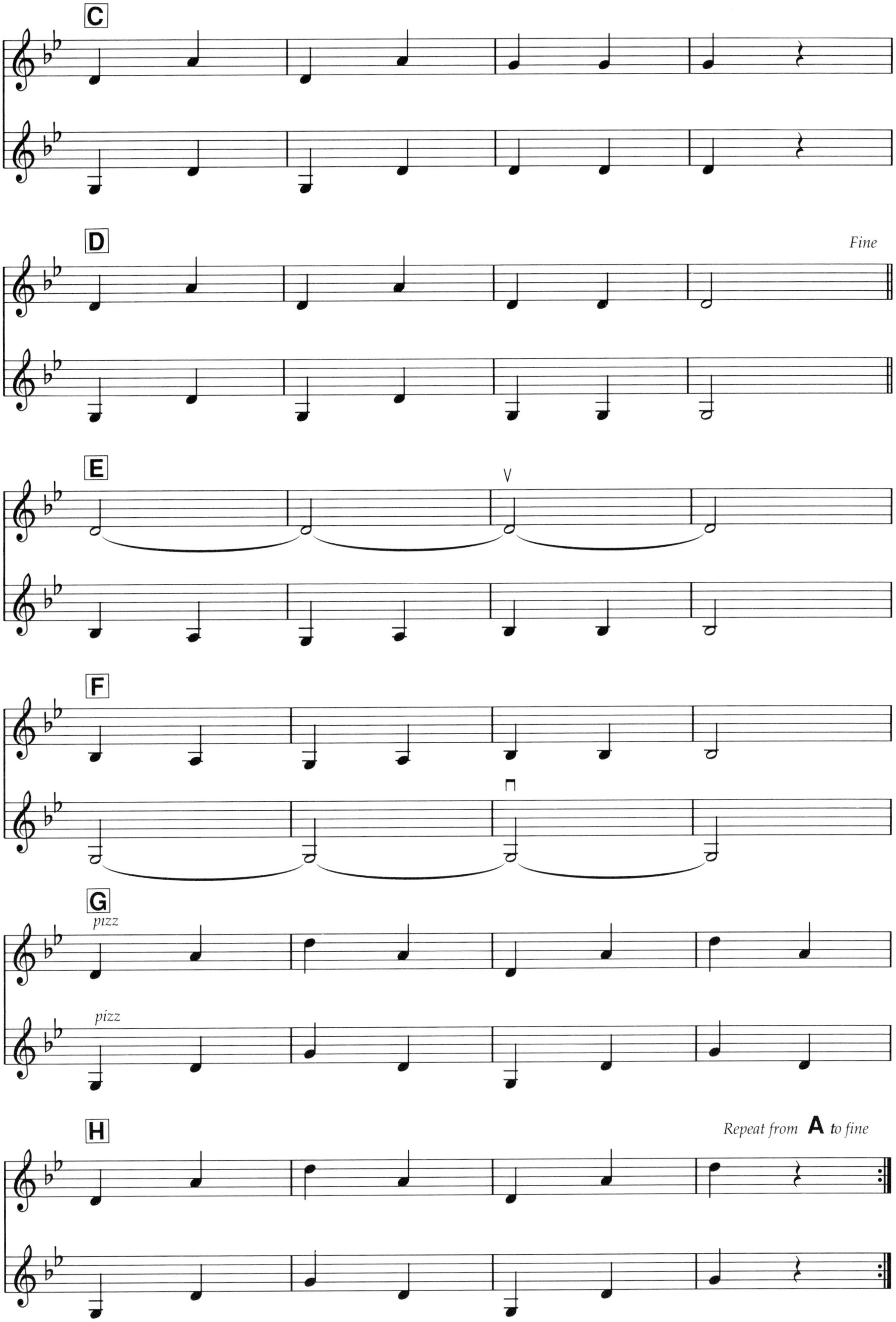
C
D
Fine
E
V
F
G
pizz
pizz
H
Repeat from A to fine

9 The Lord's my shepherd

The Lord's my shep - herd...
past - tures green he...
In
In

pas - tures green...

10 Lord of the ocean

11 Bread and fishes PART 3

As I was a walking in the springtime.......
D   D E F G F E D   E

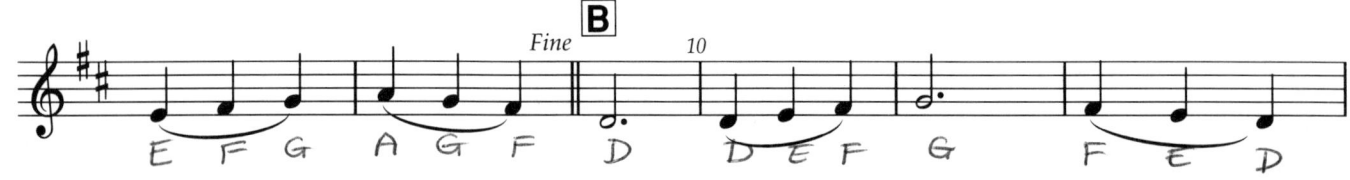

E F G A G F D   D E F G F E D

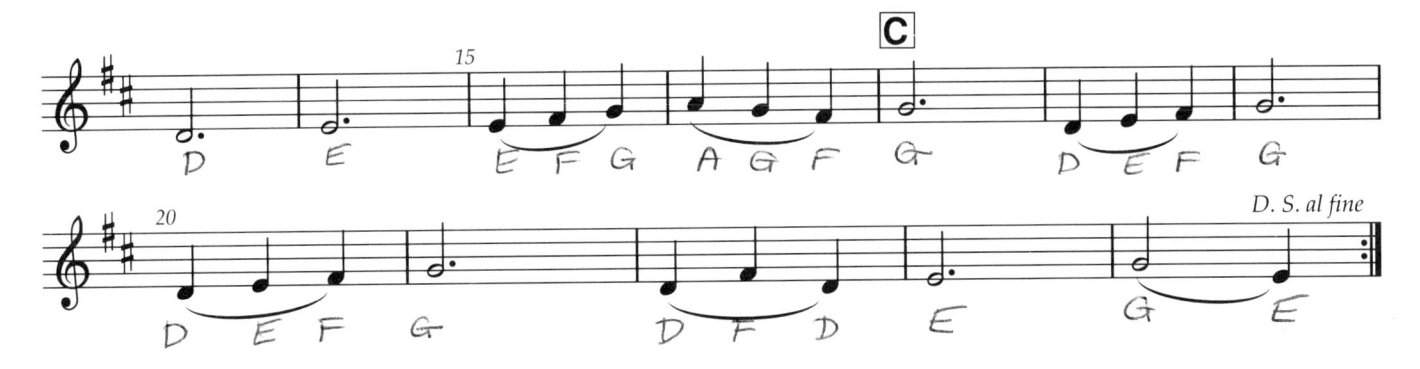

12 Sing Hosanna

13 The day thou gavest

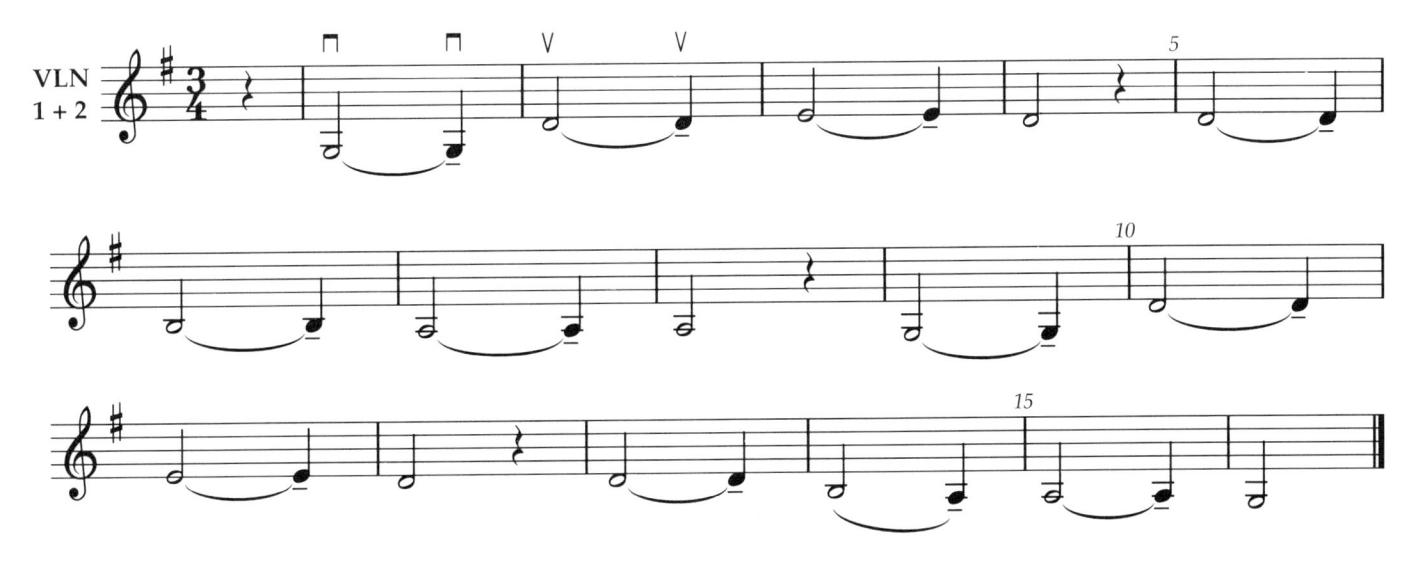

14 Make me a channel of your peace

1 Kum ba yah

PART 4 TP

Kum ba yah... Kum ba yah...
Kum ba yah... O Lord, kum ba yah.

2 Morning has broken

Morning has bro - ken...
Black - bird has spo - ken...
Praise for the sing - ing...
Praise for them, spring - ing...

© 1990, A & C BLACK (PUBLISHERS) LTD.

3 Come and praise the Lord our King

4 All things which live below the sky

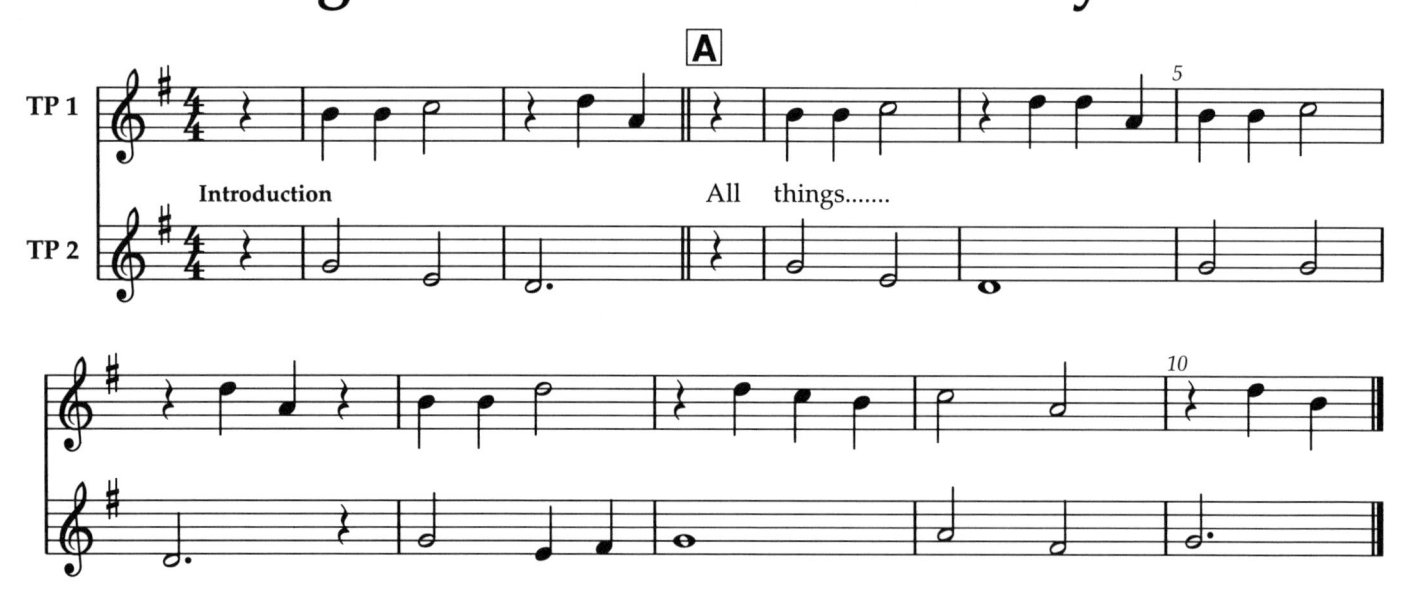

5 Every star shall sing a carol

6 Simple gifts

Introduction   'Tis the gift......

(gift to be free)

(gift to be free)

7 Lord of the harvest

8 The vine and the fig tree

Introduction And every-one be-neath the vine and fig tree...

Repeat from **A** *to fine*

9 The Lord's my shepherd

10 Lord of the ocean

11 Bread and fishes

12 Sing Hosanna

Introduction — Give me joy in my heart...

13 The day thou gavest

14 Make me a channel of your peace

Introduction

Make me a channel of your peace...

Fine

Repeat **A**

1 Kum ba yah

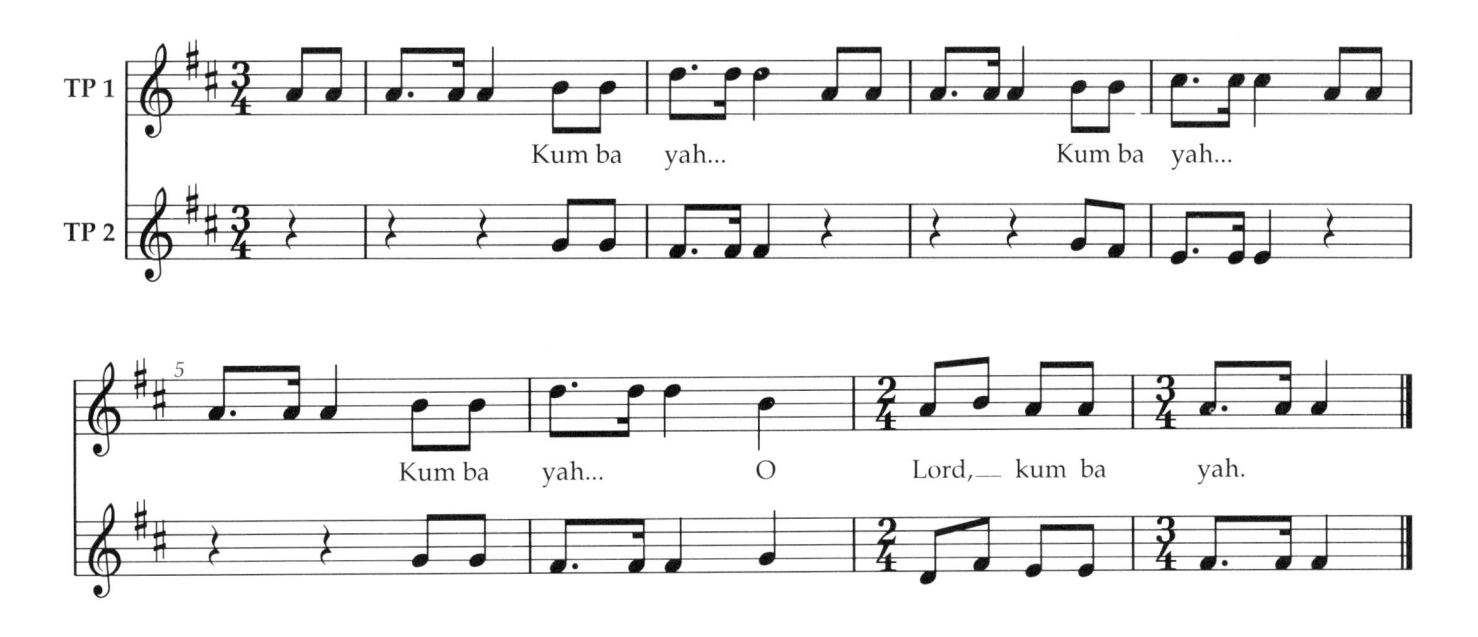

PART 4 TP

Kum ba yah... Kum ba yah... Kum ba yah... O Lord, kum ba yah.

2 Morning has broken

Morning has broken...

Blackbird has spoken...

Praise for the singing...

Praise for them, springing...

© 1990, A & C BLACK (PUBLISHERS) LTD.

3 Come and praise the Lord our King

4 All things which live below the sky

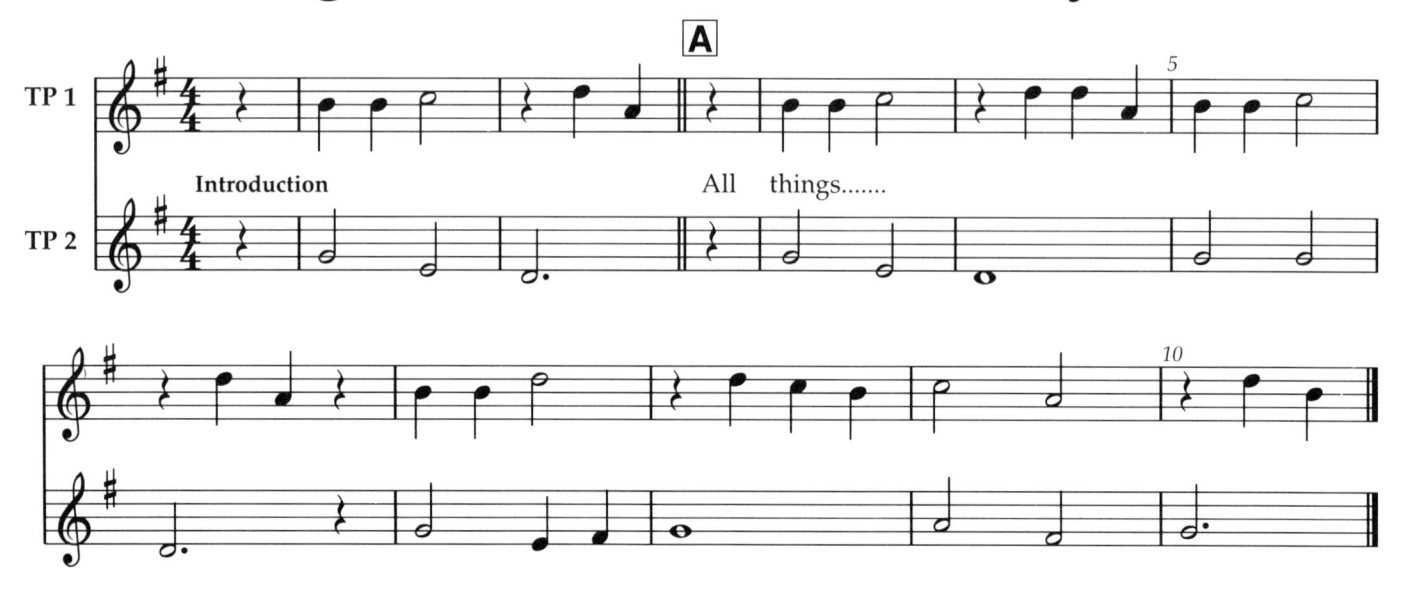

5 Every star shall sing a carol

6 Simple gifts

7 Lord of the harvest

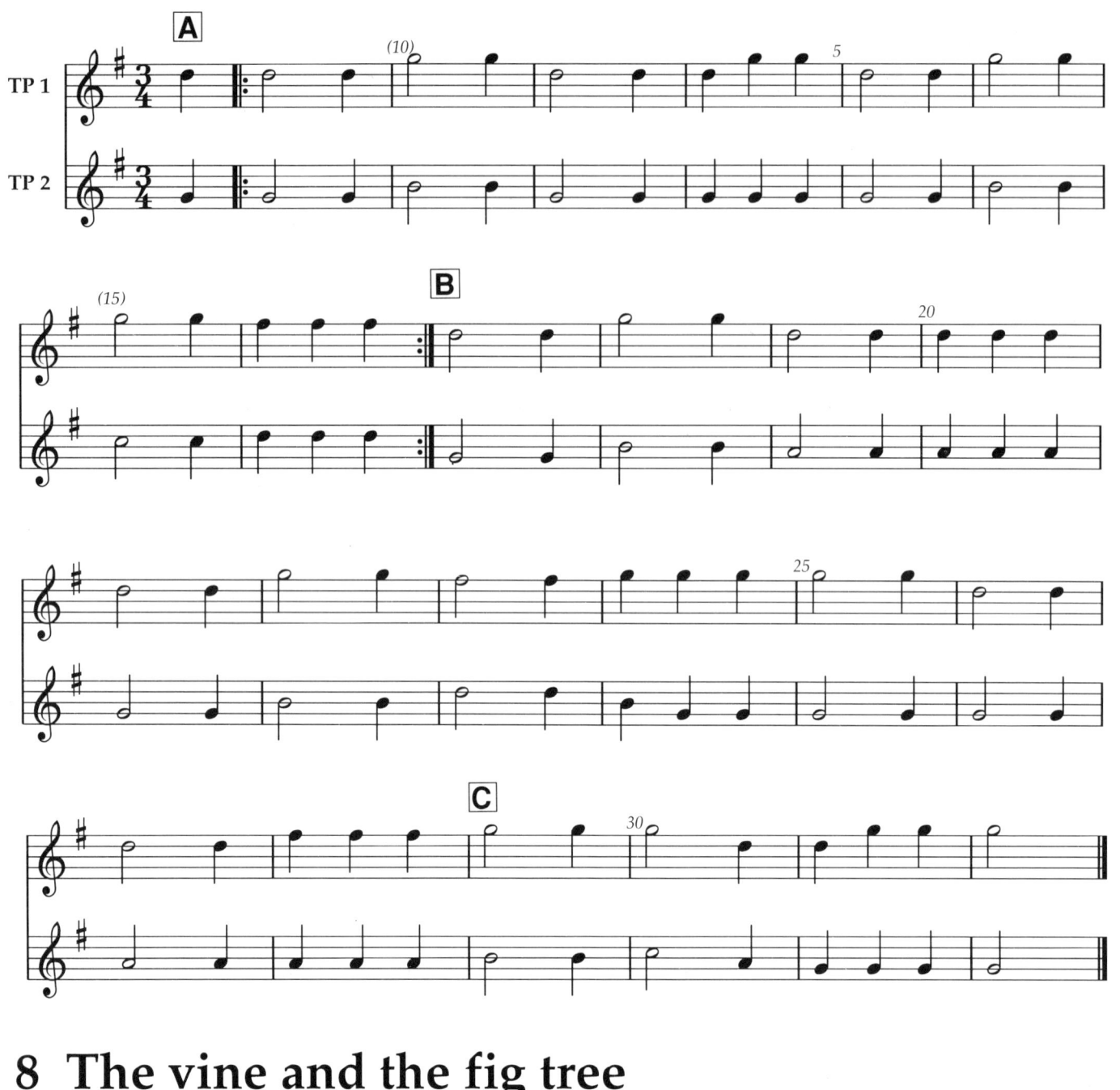

8 The vine and the fig tree

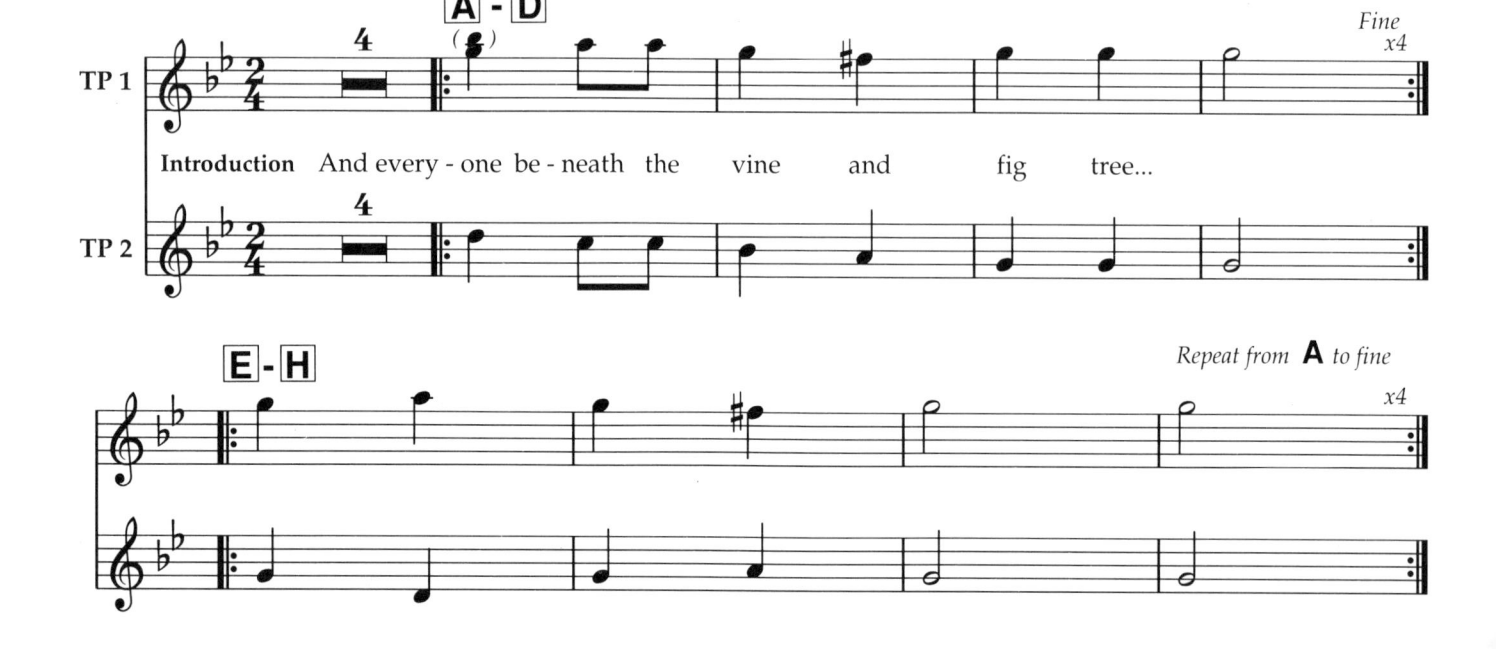

Introduction And every-one be-neath the vine and fig tree...

Repeat from **A** *to fine*

9 The Lord's my shepherd

10 Lord of the ocean

11 Bread and fishes

12 Sing Hosanna

13 The day thou gavest

14 Make me a channel of your peace

1 Kum ba yah

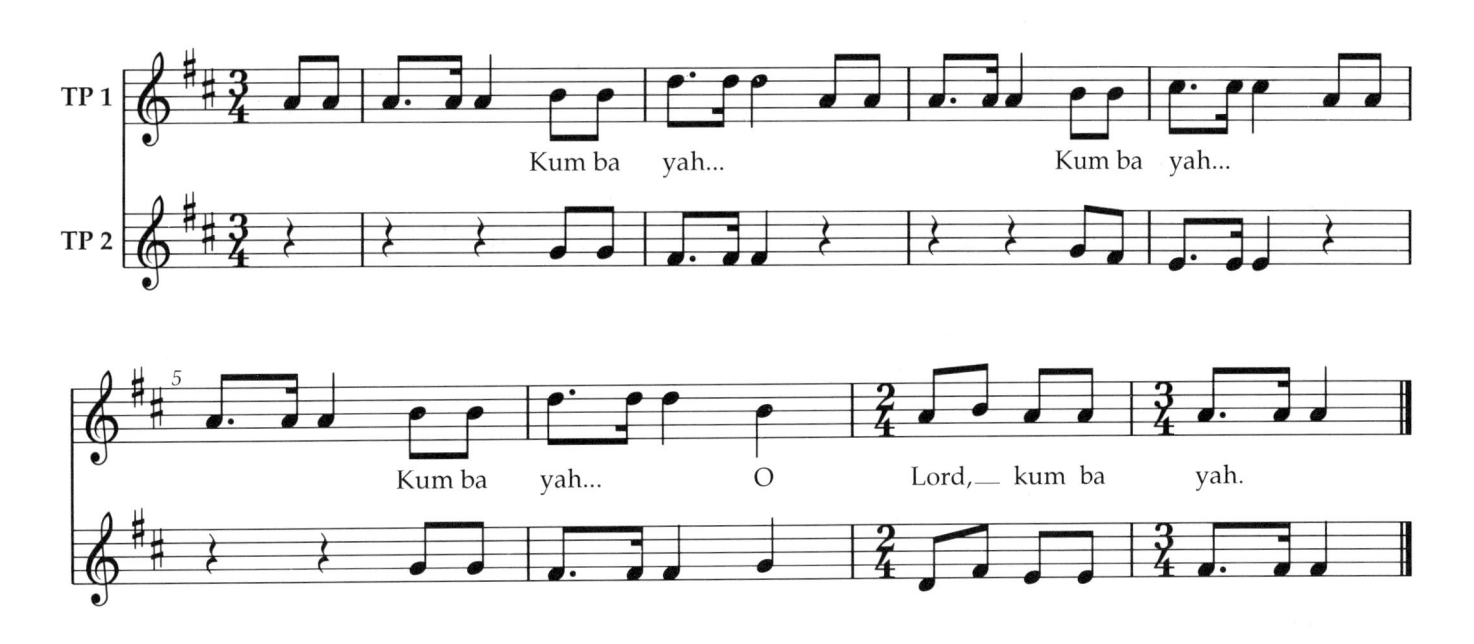

PART 4 TP

Kum ba yah... Kum ba yah... Kum ba yah... O Lord, kum ba yah.

2 Morning has broken

Morning has broken...

Blackbird has spoken...

Praise for the singing...

Praise for them, springing...

© 1990, A & C BLACK (PUBLISHERS) LTD.

3 Come and praise the Lord our King

4 All things which live below the sky

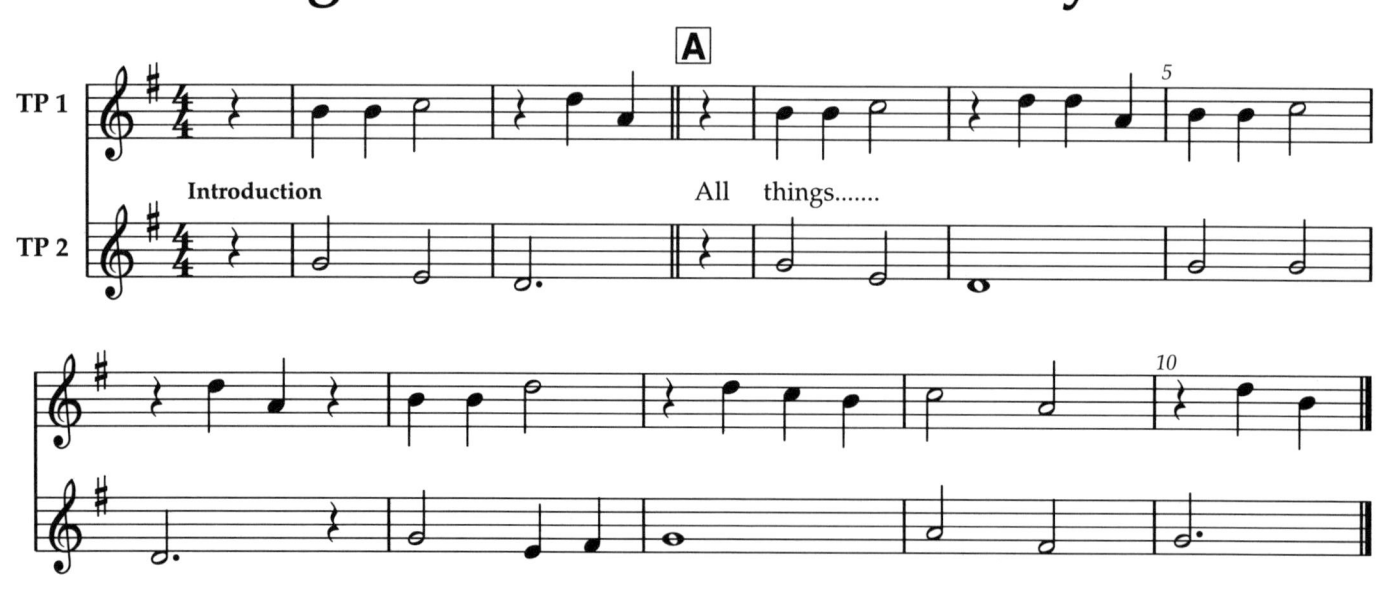

5 Every star shall sing a carol

6 Simple gifts

7 Lord of the harvest

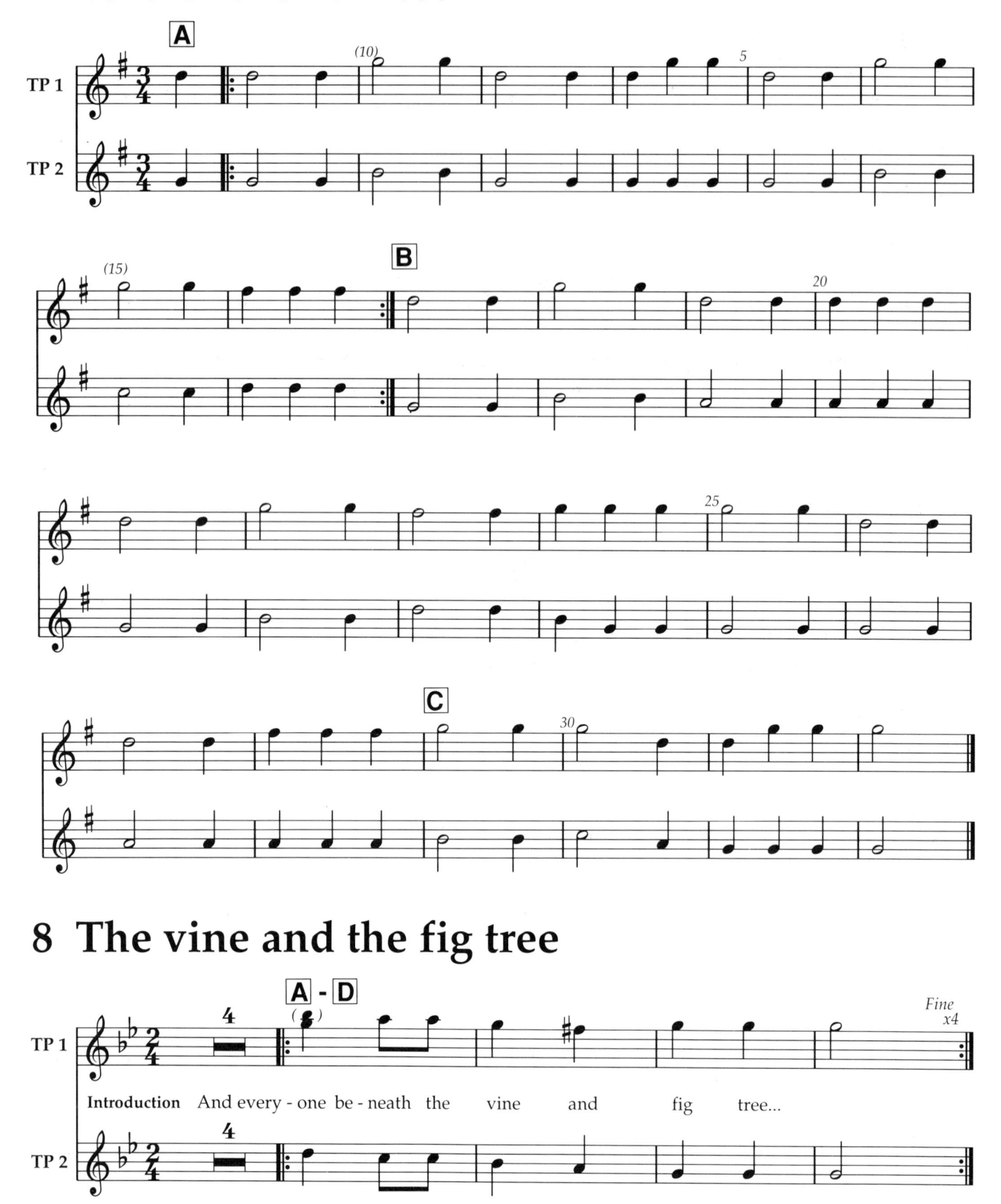

8 The vine and the fig tree

Introduction And every-one be-neath the vine and fig tree...

Repeat from **A** to fine

9 The Lord's my shepherd

10 Lord of the ocean

11 Bread and fishes

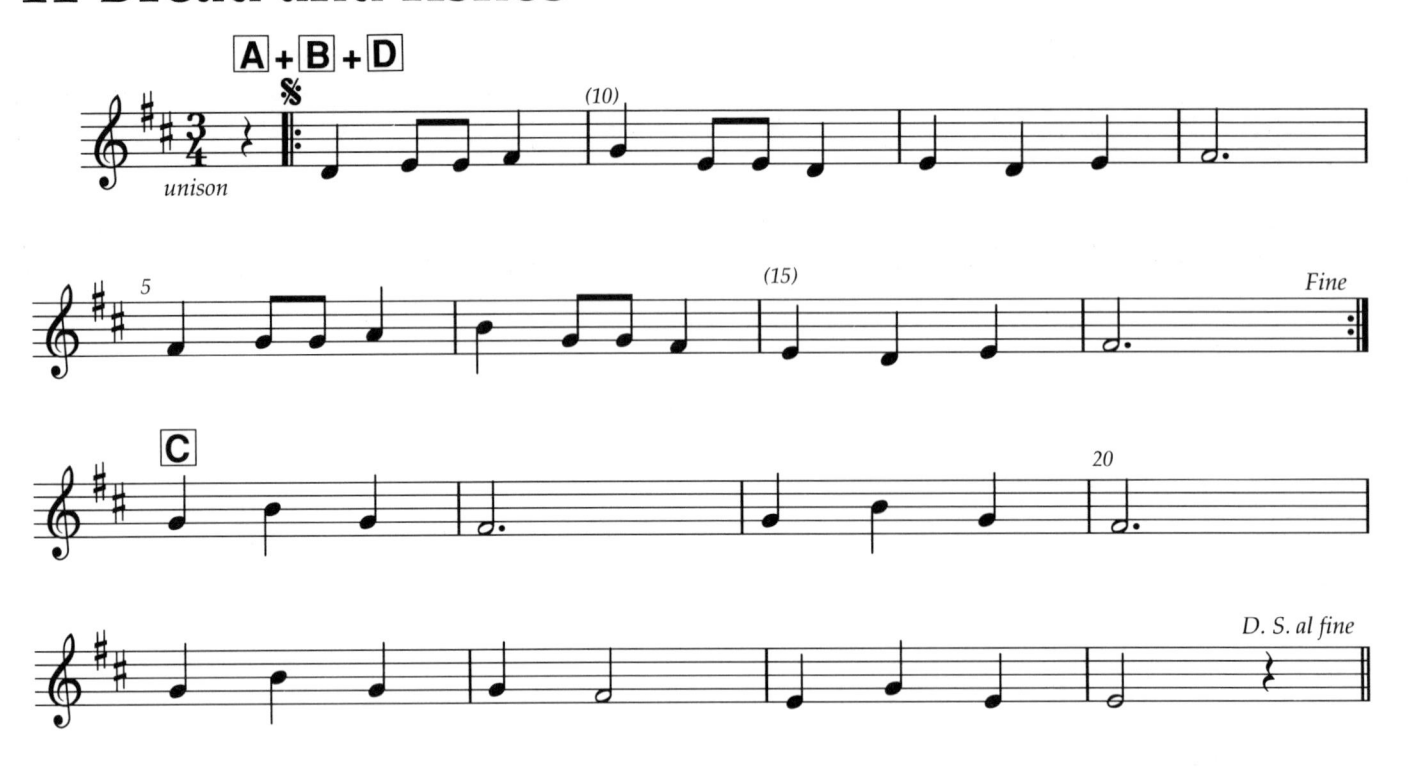

12 Sing Hosanna

13 The day thou gavest

14 Make me a channel of your peace

1 Kum ba yah

PART 5 CL/TPT

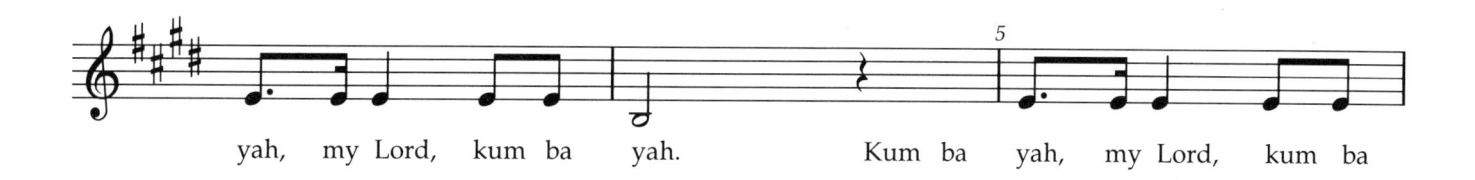

2 Morning has broken

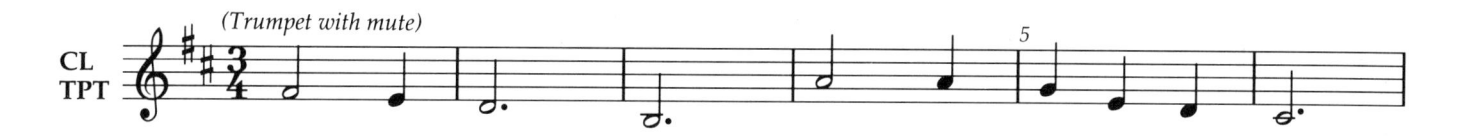

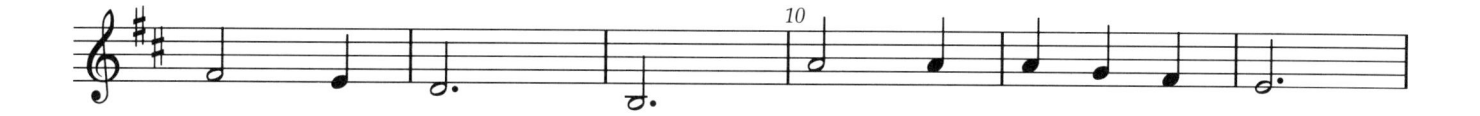

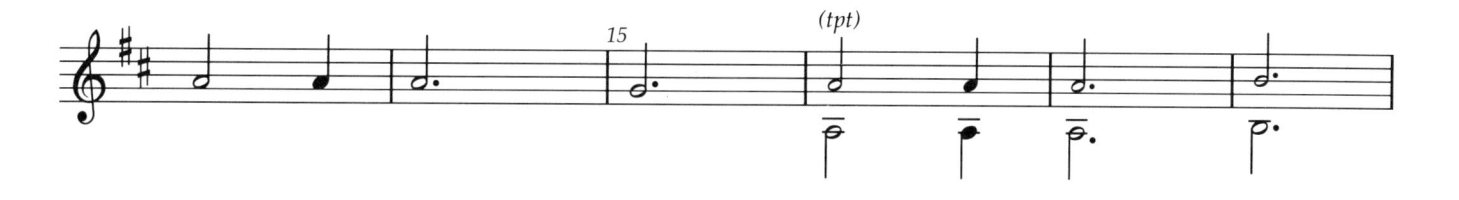

© 1990 A & C BLACK (PUBLISHERS) LTD.

3 Come and praise the Lord our King

4 All things which live below the sky

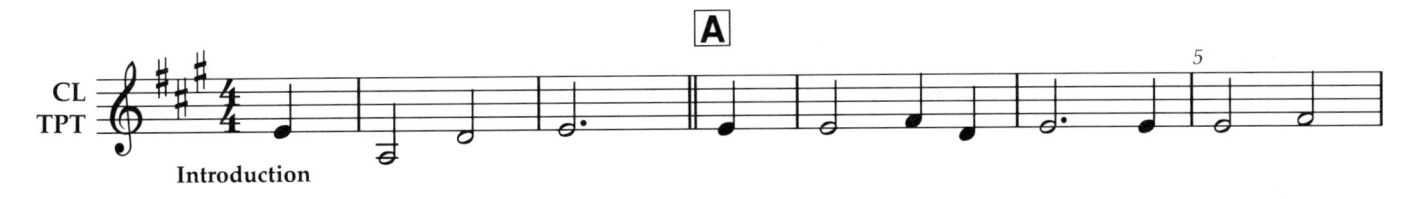

5 Every star shall sing a carol

6 Simple gifts

7 Lord of the harvest

8 The vine and the fig tree

9 The Lord's my shepherd

10 Lord of the ocean

11 Bread and fishes

12 Sing Hosanna

13 The day thou gavest

14 Make me a channel of your peace

Introduction

Make me a channel of your peace......

1 Kum ba yah

PART 6 TP/TEN CELLO

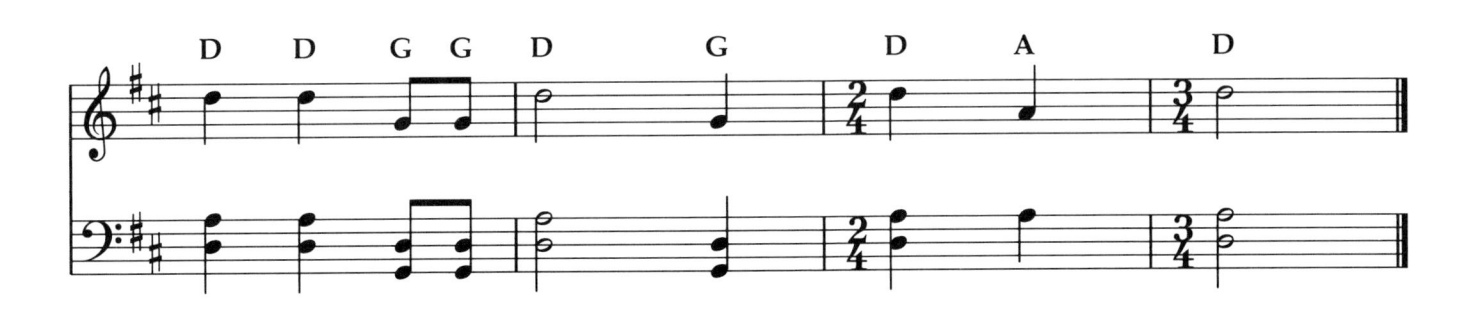

(two players, or double-stop)

Kum ba yah, my Lord, kum ba yah...

2 Morning has broken

© 1990, A & C BLACK (PUBLISHERS) LTD.

3 Come and praise the Lord our King

4 All things which live below the sky

5 Every star shall sing a carol

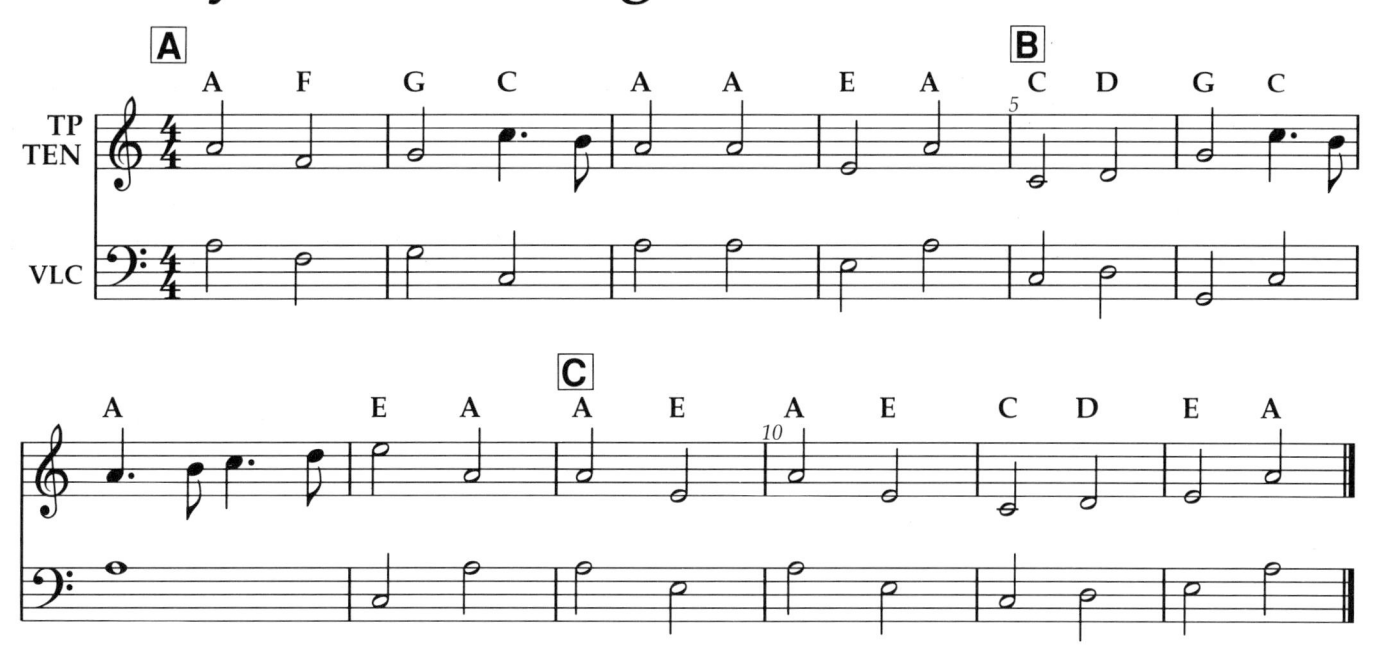

6 Simple gifts

7 Lord of the harvest

8 The vine and the fig tree

9 The Lord's my shepherd

10 Lord of the ocean

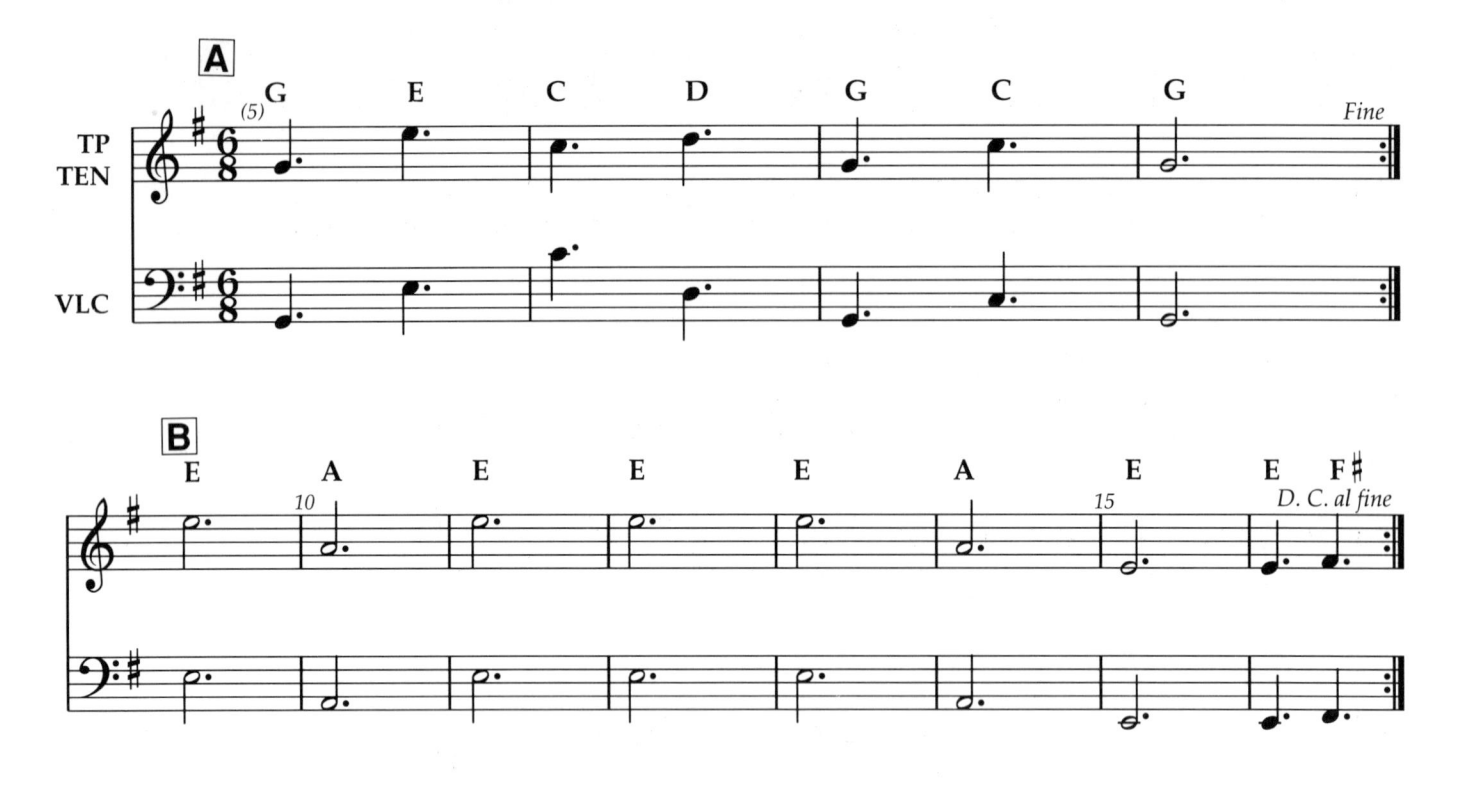

11 Bread and fishes

12 Sing Hosanna

13 The day thou gavest

14 Make me a channel of your peace

PART 6 TP/TEN CELLO

1 Kum ba yah

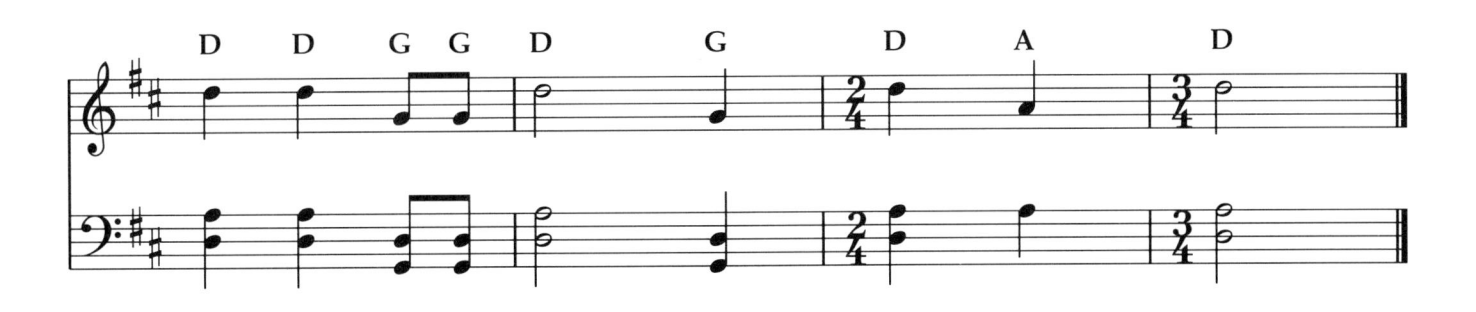

Kum ba yah, my Lord, kum ba yah...

(two players, or double-stop)

2 Morning has broken

© 1990, A & C BLACK (PUBLISHERS) LTD.

3 Come and praise the Lord our King

4 All things which live below the sky PART 6

5 Every star shall sing a carol

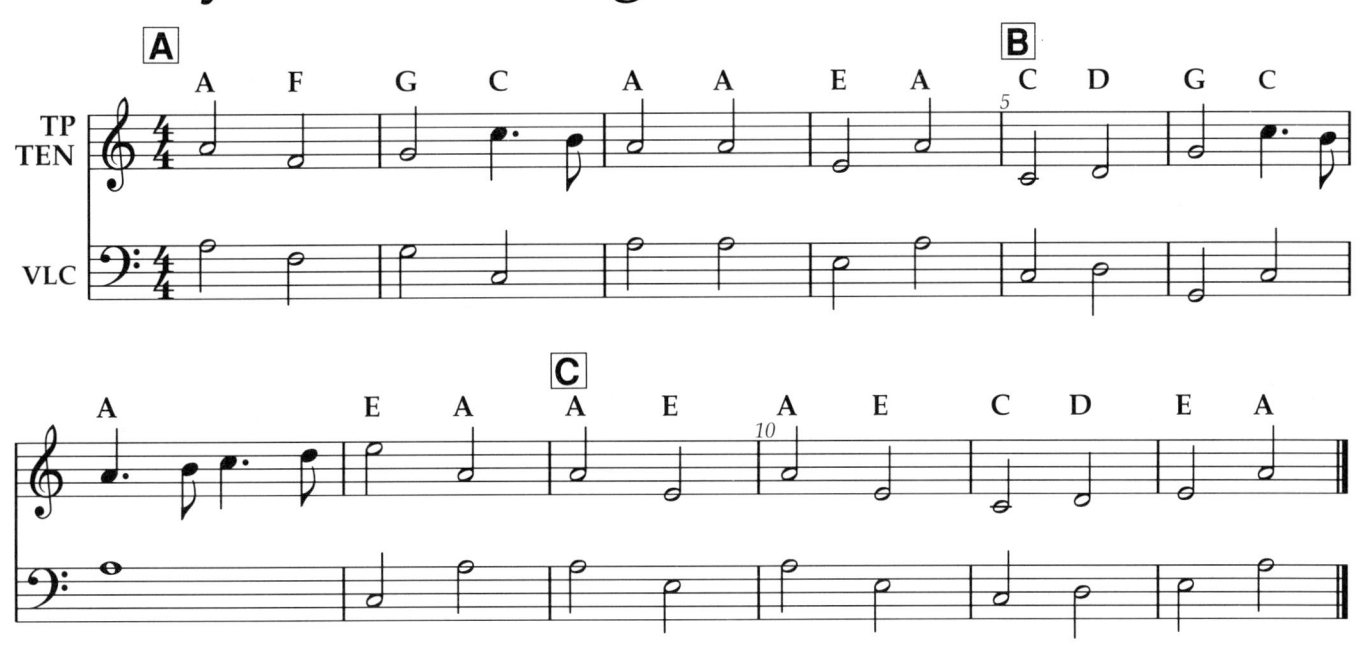

6 Simple gifts

7 Lord of the harvest

8 The vine and the fig tree

Introduction

9 The Lord's my shepherd

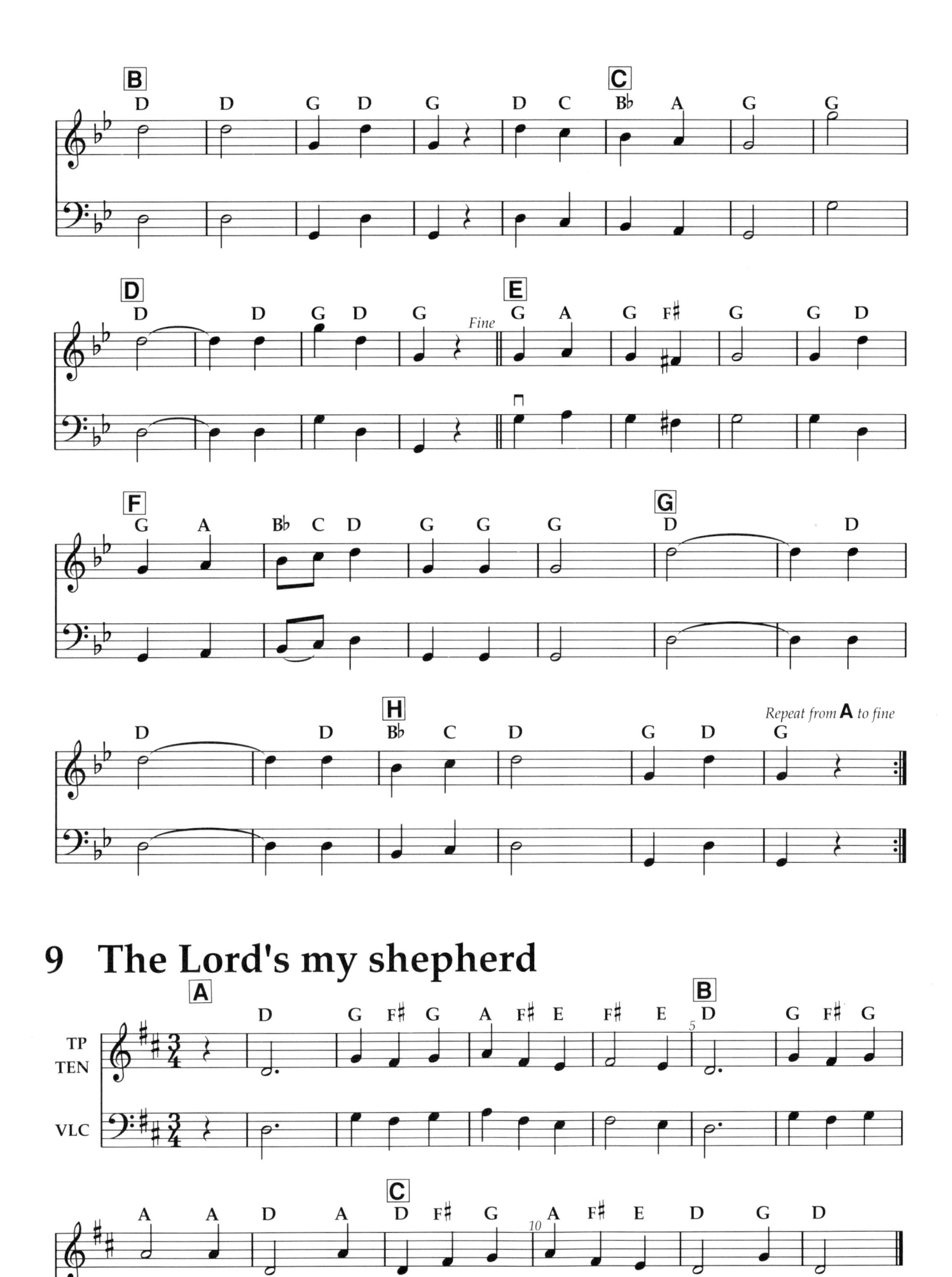

10 Lord of the ocean

11 Bread and fishes

12 Sing Hosanna

13 The day thou gavest

14 Make me a channel of your peace